First published in Great Britain by 1611 Publishing Ltd
ISBN: 9781661664213

1611 PUBLISHING Limited Reg. No. 12661918

"Any man whose errors take ten years to correct, is quite the man."

- *J Robert Oppenheimer*

WHERE I'M GOING, YOU CAN'T FOLLOW.

BY RICHARD JOHN TAYLOR

For my son, Arthur Leslie,
so you may one day read this and understand the utmost respect
and adoration I had for the man I named you after, and without
whose intervention, I would never have met your mother,
who come what may and no matter how vast the ocean between us,
will always be the love of my life.

And for Noel, without whom it would not have been possible to
complete this.

ACKNOWLEDGEMENTS

Snejana & Tanya · Tiffany, Jude, Arthur & Beckett

Richard, Rhian & Lowri · Mark & Karen

Nicholas Ball · Kev Orkian · Steve Wraith · Balvinder Singh

Simon Pearson · Brian Capron · Eleanor Bassett · Chris Langham

Jamie Wilson · Helen & Roo · Craig Gallagher · Rachel Warren

Charlie Woodward · Russell Barber · Ron Brand · Neil Drinkwater

Craig Gannon · Jeffrey Charles Richards · Sherrie Hewson

Nina Cranstoun · Jose Ubero · John & Caroline

Rula Lenska · George Thomas Mansel · Kevin Byrne

Lewis Priestman · Lacey and Frank · Pete, Gemma & Al

FOREWORD

I knew Les for a comparatively short time in later life so perhaps I got the best from this flawed, complex and fascinating man. If you have faith in rehabilitation then perhaps there is no finer example than Leslie Grantham, emerging from the dark shadow of a murder conviction and life sentence, to become a fine professional actor achieving iconic status in one of Britain's best loved soap operas with a following of millions. It's true that he had a challenging and combative personality, but I also knew this sharply observant and intelligent man to be a loyal, supportive and sometimes humble friend. He was brave in the face of a gruelling terminal illness, battling and berating it, and the people around him to the end.

The thing we had in common apart from being notorious soap villains, was that we were born in the same year and could compare and contrast the passage of our lives together. Of course, we were never short of an anecdote or joke to share, humour was our currency.

Thing about Leslie Grantham, he lingers in the mind, as I'm sure he will in yours after reading his story.

Goodbye Les, rest in peace.
Brian Capron

PROLOGUE

In 2014, a somewhat sensationalist article about me was published in a national newspaper; not a column but six full colour pages, no less. As is so often the case with these matters, people have a tendency to believe what they read in the press. It is alas, part of our psychological conditioning and human nature to retain, and more relevantly, believe things when we read them in print, more so than we would if for example, we were to hear them in a conversation, or on the radio.

It would be an understatement to say it was a stark lesson in the realities of how ruthlessly and shamelessly tabloids operate, and a rude awakening as to why one should never lie. The trouble with lying, no matter how small, justified, innocent or defensible it may seem at the time, is that when exposed, it leaves you in the vulnerable position of people being able to say whatever they want about you and it need not contain a single grain of truth. You told the first lie and thus you'll have no moral standing or defence. In an industry that already has little or no moral standing, and lies sell newspapers, you do not want to add any more fuel to the fire by being caught out in a lie you're genuinely guilty of having actually told. Quite simply, don't do it or you will find yourself, in layman's terms, the boy who cried wolf.

At the time of this 'news' breaking, I owned a wonderful little French restaurant in the heart of London's Soho. Because of its location, the majority of my patrons were either in advertising, film or somewhere in between, so naturally there were a select few regulars, namely a defamation lawyer and two journalists, who could immediately tell the article was a hatchet job and unanimously called the piece 'downright odd', to use the most polite phrasing, wondering how it had ever passed the legal department of such a seemingly respected newspaper. It contained not a single line of defence and no one I had mentioned that would willingly validate anything I was saying was contacted (because why let the truth get in the way of a good story?) and anyone that had anything bad to say, other than the person who just happened to have a new book out, naturally hid behind a pseudonym, which was ludicrous considering you only had to google the film the exposé pertained to in order to see their real names, one of whom couldn't buy me champagne quick enough upon publication, apologising and maintaining that the journalist had either twisted or completely fabricated all of his quotes.

My staff were unfortunately not as well-versed in the inner-workings of Fleet Street's 'finest' and walked out of my restaurant mid-service, almost as quickly as anyone I'd ever thought to be a friend walked out of my life, including my own family. A handful of people came to check I was okay, although their sentiment was merely a thin veil over an instinctive need to pick over the proverbial carcass for any morsel of gossip.

And then there was Leslie Grantham, more familiar with press intrusion and sensationalist journalism than anyone would ever wish or care to be. He arrived at my restaurant with the article gift wrapped and framed and instructed me to hang it pride of place behind the bar; 'If anyone comes in to have a pop, tell them if they don't like it, fuck em', or they can answer to me.'

He meant it, his demeanour that day was fiercely protective in a way I had not seen before, in person or performance. He sat in that restaurant with me for four days straight defending me against an endless stream of people akin to torch-wielding villagers in a Disney film hunting the Beast, most of whom had never even met me nor heard of me before that article, as they came to tell me exactly what they thought of me. Some of them were even taping copies of the article to the windows while others handed out copies in the market with all the passion of someone raising awareness for Oxfam. If you'd been an impartial bystander who'd never met me or Les, nor read the article, it would have been a fascinating yet disturbing study of human behaviour and proof if you ever needed it that newspapers sell and breed fear, not facts. It's a very simple, successful yet alarmingly profitable, reckless and dangerous formula for a business.

During those four days, Les and I regaled each other with our life stories and how we had both arrived at the crossroads and the milestones that we then found ourselves at. This book is largely based upon those conversations, but also on others I was fortunate enough to share with him during our twelve years of friendship, notably during a wonderful film shoot in the Lake District, somewhere that held great memories for both of us, and sadly more recent discussions on his deathbed during his final days.

Within a month, the backlash from the article and its instigator; a former employee dismissed for, among other things, ironically, selling an entirely fictitious story about Les to a tabloid, was so bad that I was forced to leave the country in very real fear for my life. Little did we know then, that this was only the beginning of a terrifying, sick and obsessive stalking ordeal against myself, and now my wife and children, that would go on for some eight years and counting, the laws inability to keep up with technology and social media failing us continually. I'd become completely detached, withdrawn, isolated and suicidal with no family, no friends, no business and no home. Everything went in one fell swoop and not even having the great Den Watts in my corner was enough to counterbalance the endless taunts of 'why are you still here, don't you understand no one wants you?' 'you deserve to rot in prison', and of course 'why don't you just do everyone a favour and kill yourself?'

Despite any misconceptions or romantic notions that I may have fled into the sunset with suitcases of cash while quaffing Dom Perignon in First Class at the expense of disgruntled investors, the reality couldn't have been more different, and I ended up sleeping rough on Venice Beach in California for nearly six months. I use the term 'sleeping' loosely as it turns out it's actually quite difficult to do so while equally unfortunate people sleeping feet away from you in the many homeless camps that plague Venice Beach at night scream endlessly, either from drug withdrawals, drug highs or from simple madness; an alarming portion of Los Angeles homeless community is made up of dangerous former mental hospital inmates who were discharged in 1967 when President Reagan signed the Lanterman-Petris-Short Act, ending the institutionalization of patients against their will. 'Humbling' isn't an appropriate word. It was, put bluntly, a horrific experience I will carry with me forever and taught me that whether I have a roof over my head, or merely a sleeping bag, I will always be grateful for either, because it will invariably never be that bad again, and god forbid it is, I know I've lived through it before and I came out the other side.

Fortunately, Les hadn't given up on me, then, nor ever. He put a down payment on a small apartment, got me cleaned up and in doing so, afforded me the opportunity to get a job doing an honest day's work and get back on my feet. Without his intervention, I have no doubt in my mind I'd have taken my own life. Les was my biggest champion and behind closed doors rescued me from my darkest times. He helped me out when everyone else had closed their doors, turned their backs and hidden under their tables. Those times, without him, would have ended very differently and very tragically.

Les attended many a dinner at my home in London, where we'd stay up talking until sunrise, yet we were equally comfortable in each other's silence reading scripts or writing a treatment while working our way to the bottom of a Malbec. We shared our love of a good red, of *Casablanca* and of Bogart, we shared deep routed insecurity and shared a love of good writing. We shared a mutual appreciation and respect for the art of television production, a subject on which his knowledge was arguably only surpassed by that of his mentor, *EastEnders* creator Julia Smith. We also knew the worst things about each other and that was okay. Les and I have both destroyed people's lives, we've both made *incredibly* stupid mistakes and by god have we paid, and we continue to pay. But we always held our hands up to our mistakes and despite public perception, there has never been a day when either of us hasn't thought of what we have done and felt crippled by grief, shame, regret or remorse. One of the qualities I admired most about him was his honesty and humbleness about his past and his shortcomings. As Les would say, 'of course I have regrets, but you can't go around wearing a hair shirt all your life or you'd never get out of bed. I fucked up, now I'm going to move on.'

The naysayers would naturally argue we don't deserve to move on, but Les and I were bound by our faults, our grief and by our profound understand that no one is perfect. We're all human. Everybody fucks up and people deserve a second chance. We were furthermore united by our knowledge that you should never believe what you read in a newspaper – ever – many a better man than myself or Les has had his life ruined because there was simply nothing else to write that day. Yes, they really do just make it up. This is as much a cautionary tale as it is a memoir – beware if you chose to court the press; if you're very lucky they will build you up first but regardless, they will destroy you. We live in a primitive time where anyone can write something on Twitter with no evidence and the next day it's the solid basis for a Daily Mail article; a contributing factor I'm sure, as to why Wikipedia will no longer consider the Daily Mail a citable source. There is no such thing as free speech and forgiveness has no place in a world of trial by social media. You can lose your job over an ill-advised comment you made a decade ago, no matter how much you may have grown, learnt or changed since. These headlines rile the public to bay for blood, calling for people to never work again, to be imprisoned, to be driven to suicide, all of which sell more newspapers. It is the definition of cutthroat in its purist form. Unfortunately, suing a newspaper is a very drawn out, risky, expensive and complicated process and unless you have more money than them, which you invariably don't, then you're just pissing in the wind. Part of you will wish it was personal so you can find some reasoning or sense in it, but there is none, it's just business. As the News of the World journalist Paul McMullen infamously said when defending phone hacking on *Newsnight*, he always found ruining people's lives 'kind of fun'. It's as simple as that, they're paid handsomely to do it and you will never win.

Grief is a terrible, horrible thing. Writing this book has been one of the most painful experiences of my life, yet it was one of the most cathartic. It hurts deeply to imagine moving forward in my life, both personally and professionally, without Les's frequent words of encouragement and touching notes. Even if short of time or on different time zones, he always found a moment for the obligatory 'if they don't like it…'

Although it weighed heavily on my heart, I felt touched to have been someone he confided in when he received his first diagnosis, and to have been there in his last days as he privately but gallantly battled harder and braver than anyone I've known for nearly three years against his cancer.

When he was told he wasn't going to win this fight and his time left would be so much shorter than we'd imagined or planned for, his reaction and subsequent composure during his final days were the epitome of dignity and a harrowing lesson in courage and acceptance. More so, even then, he was still full of his wicked, sharp sense of humour and charm, far greater than that of the legendary character he made so famous.

Publicly, he will always be remembered as one of the most iconic characters of all time, responsible for an episode of *EastEnders* that still to this day holds the highest viewing figure of any episode of a British television programme ever.

Personally, he will always be loved and respected by me, not only as the most professional and consummate actor I have worked with, but more importantly the most wickedly funny, generous, kind, compassionate and understanding, empathetic man I have had the privilege to know. The firstborn of my twins was named Arthur Leslie to acknowledge the insurmountable gratitude I had for his unfaltering support of me.

He imparted to me and shared the sentiments of several other well-known actors and mutual friends that have suffered at the hands of both press intrusion, and of mistakes of our own doing; that picking yourself up after a setback, whether you deserved that setback or not, is inevitably hard but that isn't a good enough reason to give up. Don't excuse or justify yourself to anyone and don't bring others down in order to feel content. Trust no one in our industry. Just tell the truth, because it's a lot easier to remember. Never get caught up in self-congratulation. Act out of nothing but good intention, even if people didn't have the foresight to see it immediately, because in time, they will. Be patient. Be yourself, everyone else is taken. Be good to your children, it's the only thing that will matter in the end. Live well and have no relationship with the people who hate you, you'll be much happier for it. Trying to persuade them to think better of you would bring them back into your life and your time is too short and your talent too great to waste on that.

At a screening of a film we made together, a journalist asked Les how he'd like to one day be remembered and he poignantly replied, 'as someone who got out of the gutter.'

Les achieved that, he saved my life, and surpassed so much more. With that in mind, I shall not keep you from him any longer...

CHAPTER ONE

George Tyler, a thirty-six-year-old taxi driver had picked up a fare from his hometown in Birmingham, collecting him from the taxi rank just outside New Birmingham Street Station at 10:15 p.m. Witnesses described the passenger, who requested to travel to Burton, as being in his mid-twenties, dark hair, clean shaven and well presented in an RAF uniform. In the small hours of the following morning, but a hundred yards from the canal bridge at Clay Mills on the Staffordshire-Derbyshire border, residents heard a loud bang, but spotting nothing other than Tyler's car, merely assumed it had broken down. A few hours later, PC Erin Challinor came across the vehicle and upon investigating discovered Tyler's deceased body; he'd been shot four times before being moved to the back of the taxi, where he had bled out and subsequently died.

This is one of two notable events that occurred on 30th April 1947, however, the second would not make national headlines. A few hours after the discovery of Tyler's body, one hundred and fifty miles south at 14 Flodden Road, Camberwell SE5, Adelaide Victoria Grantham gave birth to her third child, Leslie Michael.

Adelaide's first child, Matthew, had the misfortune of falling victim to a fatal chest infection shortly after his birth. He had been named after Captain Matthew Finders, from whom she had claimed to have been a direct descendant.

Les's father, Walter William Grantham, had been one of the first to have volunteered, having already been a member of the local branch of the Territorial Army, whose barracks were conveniently located at the end of their road. Originally joining as a Royal Fusilier, he had quickly risen to the decorated rank of a colour sergeant. 'He was one of the thousands at Dunkirk where he bravely spent nearly two days in the water waiting for the boats to turn up and rescue them; 'They were real heroes,' Les proudly recalled.

Upon returning home, he was stationed at Shorncliffe Barracks in Essex where he would become an instructor to new recruits. His duties included training them how to correctly throw a hand grenade; one day, he was guiding a group through the standard procedure and took a grenade from its box and it exploded without warning with the pin still intact. Two of his recruits were killed; 'Dad survived but was unfortunate enough to wake up the next morning in the military hospital with his right arm gone below the elbow. The aftercare was a bit primitive by today's standards, they basically showed him how to slice a loaf of bread with his left hand instead...'

When his dad was subsequently discharged from the army, he took up a position at Boots, where he would later meet Adelaide. He remained at Boots for some four decades; 'He loved it there, he took so much pride in it, he was secretary of all the staff social clubs, always organizing something, whether it was the Christmas party or a dinner dance. We hardly saw him then, he'd work Monday to Saturday, gone before six and never home before half seven.'

After a whirlwind romance, Walter and Adelaide married and as a result of the post-war baby boom it wasn't long before the arrival of Les's older brother John; Les was to be born two years later, and what a year 1947 was; *A Miracle on 34th Street* stormed box offices worldwide, the Treaty of Dunkirk was signed, the Thames flooded, the government nationalised the coal industry and Princess Elizabeth announced her engagement to one Lieutenant Phillip Mountbatten.

At a time when entire towns were popping up on any spare corner of London, Walter decided to move his growing brood to a brand-new council house in St Paul's Cray, Kent.

The house they moved to was on Clarendon Road; coincidentally the television studios in where Les would later go on to become one of the most famous household names in Britain were also located on Clarendon Road, albeit another by the same name in Elstree some forty miles north west of their home.

When Les's sister Angela was born, the family moved again, a mere staggering distance to a bigger house where the family was completed by the arrival of his brother Phillip. Les had fond memories of his time at this particular house, namely hearing on the wireless that Everest had been conquered and along with the rest of the neighbourhood, cramming into the only house with a television to watch the Queen's Coronation in 1953, followed by the most wonderful street party; 'At the time this one old girl was not just the only owner of a television set on the estate, but one of the few to own a car so we thought she was a millionaire even though she lived in a council house on the same estate as the rest of us.'

After the Coronation, Walter, along with every other person across the country, invested in their own television set; 'Dad's new nightly ritual would always be watching the telly, then he would get up out of his chair, take off his false hand and set it down in its spot, wind up the old clock we had and then it was up to bed.'

Boots were good to the Grantham family, as Walter was able to bring home anything they stocked for wholesale price and in the winter, he'd even bring discarded crates to put on the fire and save on the cost of coal, still at an all-time high, post-war. The wage Walter brought home would cover the family's food, the gas and the electricity and then of a Wednesday, Adelaide would draw his war pension from the local post office, which would cover the rent and whatever else might be owed to 'the seemingly never-ending line of tallymen knocking on the door. We seemed forever to live on the tick and when money was low, they'd always have a row. He was convinced he'd left her enough to cover everything and naturally she disagreed.'

Les attended a Church of England school and when he started, he had been ambidextrous; his teacher would regularly hit him hard with a ruler when he attempted to use his preferred left hand to write with; 'I reckon she believed only the devil's disciples were left-handed.'

In what could be interpreted as one of his earliest acting roles, Les decided to feign illness to escape the ruler and when his mum inquired as to why he didn't wish to go in, he showed her the bruises and as soon as his dad arrived home, he was informed. Walter took the day off work to attend a meeting with the teacher in an attempt to broker some kind of peace deal but when the teacher denied any wrongdoing, Les produced his wounded hand, to which the teacher remarked he must have been in a playground scuffle. It was quickly apparent to Walter, who didn't suffer fools gladly, that she was lying and he and Adelaide decided it was time to move schools; 'I bloody hated having to put up with her for the rest of that term, she'd belted me and then lied about it. She'd make these snide remarks and eventually I became terrified of using my left hand. She'd literally beaten it out of me.'

Happy at his new school, on the way home Les would often pass a little corner shop with an orchard backing onto it, obviously tempting to all the local children who would climb over the fence and knock apples and plums down at any chance they could; 'Whenever you had to go buy something from the corner, my mum would tell me to bring home any apples I could find, although one time I was doing it and fell out of the tree and caught my back on an old iron bed frame. I went home looking like the walking wounded but all mum wanted to know was where the fruit was.'

The Grantham family moved once again, this time to St Mary Cray on the other side of the railway, where they were finally blessed with a garden; 'Dad loved that garden, although Christ knows what it looked like to the neighbours watching a one-armed man dig a vegetable patch!'

On Saturdays, Les and John would go with their dad to the sports ground in New Eltham where they would watch the Boots team play either cricket, a sport Les developed a life-long love for. Away from the arguments at home, Walter was a different man, who Les said was adored and respected by his colleagues.

When Les was around thirteen, the drivers at Boots were due to go on strike, which worried Walter somewhat. Les said Walter was very much a 'don't rock the boat' man, and a great believer in the establishment. At Christmas, Adelaide and the children would always have to keep quiet during the Queens speech. So, the thought of a strike made Walter feel pretty out of his comfort zone; the day of the strike meeting arrived and after a somewhat melodramatic speech from the shop steward, Walter stood up and declared that sod everyone else, he had four kids to feed. The strike never came to fruition.

Walter would arrive home at the same time every evening, but Les remembers one night, again with pride, when he was so late that even Adelaide was worried. Without a phone back then, there was little else to do but worry, especially when the wireless announced a huge train crash in Lewisham. Later that evening... much later, Walter was returned to the Grantham residence in the back of a police car, but fortunately not having been arrested. He'd been waiting at the station when the announcement about the crash was made. Quick as a flash, he commandeered the station master's phone and was co-ordinating between the police and the emergency services making sure drugs were despatched to the hospitals to cope with the influx of people; 'After that, Boots had a phone installed for us but we were only allowed to use it for incoming calls so we'd still have to walk down to the phone box on the corner of the road to call anyone. We were under orders from dad not to tell anyone we had the thing, so we didn't have to turn down neighbours wanting to use it, but I reckon the wire from the telephone pole to our house was probably a bit of a giveaway.'

The Grantham's would regularly holiday in Leysdown, Camber Sands and on one occasion Blackpool; 'I don't remember much about that one other than it being grey, and I'm still haunted by the memory of my beach ball blowing away the minute I stepped off the train.'

There was always a competition to see which of the children could see the sea first. The seaside was wonderful, and he loved everything from the candyfloss to the arcades and the sights and sounds of holidaymakers escaping for even a weekend. Given the family was six strong, they'd often stay in caravans and the children would be up and out the door as soon as they woke; 'Anything to escape that smell of those wet towels.'

While the rest of the family would stick together, Les would often wander off by himself. His dad had always said he was 'away with the other', in his own world. One day, while walking the boardwalk and passing the usual entertainment of Punch and Judy and knobbly knee competitions, Les spotted a sign for a junior talent competition, and on a whim and with no thought as to what his actual talent might be, decided to enter. Les confided in his dad that evening that he'd entered but had no idea what he was supposed to do; 'Make 'em laugh!' were Walter's pearls.

Les devoured several joke columns in his favourite comics and when it came to his turn on stage, he took a deep breath and went through the motions. No one laughed other than the Grantham family, 'clearly over-compensating as a rogue beach ball blew across the stage like a tumbleweed, no doubt the same one I'd lost when I got off the train. I took a bow and tripped right over the microphone cable… at least that got a bloody laugh.'

Indeed, so much of a laugh that it secured his place in the next round, but sadly his jokes were still dire and that's as far as he got. Despite not winning, his first experience of laughter and applause made him want more. Encouraging his interest, Walter gave Les a set of stage make-up for Christmas, something he would treasure for years to come; 'He'd never have dreamed I'd have ended up on stage in any capacity, but that present was a huge factor in reinforcing my love of dressing up and playing parts.'

Les spent many an hour performing in his room, although those solitary performances brought more satisfaction than he would receive the next time he appeared in front of an audience as the shepherd in the school Nativity play. The direction was simple; point in wonder at the bright star in the distance. The cast followed these instructions to the letter, with the exception of Les, who was looking in awe in the opposite direction.

When things were tight, day trips to seaside resorts on the southern coast were no less appreciated, albeit the atmosphere between Walter and Adelaide slightly strained. It didn't help that unable to get his arm wet, all Walter could do was sit and watch the frivolities.

Walter was beginning to suffer bad pain in his teeth, accompanied by some rather unsightly boils on his neck. Even for a smoker, Les remembered what a great set of teeth he had. The dentist could find nothing wrong with either him or his teeth, but eventually the pain was unbearable, and his teeth were removed. As the dentist had originally said, there was absolutely nothing wrong with his teeth but was with his gums; when the grenade had exploded, shrapnel had entered his body and over years had travelled through his system and ended up in his neck, hence the boils and deteriorating gums. Years later, he'd have half of his stomach removed because of further contamination.

When Les was in the midst of his eleven-plus, Walter and Adelaide welcomed their fifth child, Simon, who had the misfortune to be born without his kidneys. Although enraptured with his new baby brother, Les still sat his exams but after, was called into the headmaster's office. Les's only contact with the headmaster prior to that day had been to receive a telling off, but this day Les noted he adopted a more caring and sensitive disposition. He broke Les's heart when he informed him that Simon had passed away ten days ago but he and his parents had decided to keep the news from him until after the exams.

As Les moved onward and upward to St Mary Cray Secondary Modern, known locally as Herne's Rise, he was concerned he would be judged based upon the antics of his older brother, John. Having regularly played truant and simply refused to carry on at Dartford Technical School, John been moved to Herne's Rise a couple of years earlier. Les's fears were correct and by the time he arrived at Herne's Rise, his brother had already left quite the reputation and the teachers already had his card marked. He and his sister were warned in no uncertain terms that they were under a watchful eye. His first day was a rocky one and he hated it, not because of the lessons but because of the tiresome and seemingly endless remarks about John. It wasn't long before he began playing truant himself and hanging out at mates' houses. When he was at school, he was caned regularly for his lack of attendance; 'The deputy headmaster would call it six of his best, but I can assure you there was nothing particularly great about any of them.'

More often truant than not, Les took a job at the local greengrocers on his horse and cart round. He also had a Saturday job at the local bread factory; 'We'd grab the van as it dropped the papers at local paper shop and hitch a lift down the Bridge House pub where we would jump off and then walk the rest of the way to the bread factory. We'd wait outside until the drivers left, then they'd pick a boy they wanted to help and off we went. In the beginning you'd shout out 'want a boy, mister?' in the hope of being picked up.'

One Christmas, Les and the other local lads were loading up the vans for the next day's rounds when the factory caught fire. This was the day before Christmas Eve so all the lads worked into the small hours of the morning shifting barrows full of Christmas puddings and bread out of being baked twice; 'I call that one the year I saved Christmas', Les recounted with a smile and one of Den's winks.

Les's relationship with his mother began to decline fairly early. One weekend, his uncle was visiting for Sunday lunch and Les had been cleaning out a van, so when he popped his head in the house to say hello looking like he'd just come down the chimney, Adelaide exploded with anger. His uncle attempted to diffuse the situation, which promptly descended into a full-scale argument. By the time the food was ready, Les had been banished to his room and his uncle had gotten back in his car and gone home.

Les said that Adelaide's own mother had been equally hard to please. She would make the pilgrimage from her house in Hertfordshire once a year to visit and Les couldn't recall any of those trips being a joyous occasion. No matter how hard he would try to please her, he'd usually end up being ordered to leave the house or go to his room. Les felt that his mother, like her mother before her, had always carried an air of disappointment with her, as though she had been destined for better things and that she viewed children as an inconvenience, some sort of ever-present reminder that a woman was no longer in her prime.

Les described his final year of school as 'easy, to say the least', most likely on account of him hardly being there, yet despite that, he still managed to be elected house captain. As one might expect, the housemaster had tried to order a re-vote, but it was futile, although Les said he really needn't have bothered as his career in politics lasted all of twenty-four hours, when after leaving school, he could barely make it to the gate before lighting up a cigarette and the housemaster promptly leapt from out from behind a tree, hauling him before the headmaster the very next morning, and that was the end of that.

From its humble beginnings as a radio show, *The Huggett's* had been turned into several films starring Jack Warner, and so when the Huggett family moved into Les's local pub, the Seven Stiles, it was only right that Jack Warner of *Dixon of Dock Green* fame was asked to attend the grand opening, a star-studded affair; even his brother John managed to end up in the local newspaper beside Jack Warner himself.

All the locals adored Harry and Ada Huggett. John wasted little time in getting a job behind the bar, but they also took Les under their wing. It was during this first stint behind a bar, that Les inevitably became friendly with many of the locals, including a young chap by the name of John. They quickly became thick as thieves and when Les recounted the first story involving John, I couldn't help but see some sort of foreshadowing, but I know Les thought nothing of it, and probably rightly so. John had invited Les to his sister's wedding and as they were waiting for the bride and grooms' pictures to be taken the police had burst into the churchyard and stormed straight over to John's uncle. When they grabbed him, an object had gone up and flying through the air, eventually landing at Les's feet; 'I looked down and saw this gun. It must have been raining because the grass was wet, so I stood on it and pushed it down into the earth as much as I could while everyone else was still making a commotion. As the police were dragging John's uncle away, his mother came over to me and I told her it was taken care of. She grabbed me and had me out of there quicker than one of those bakers looking for a boy!'

Finally hanging up his school uniform, John secured a fifteen-year-old Les a job at Burroughs Wellcome as a junior laboratory technician making sheep inoculations. He was, as most would be, unprepared for the sight of men in white coats swinging mice by their tails, smashing their heads against tables and then cremating them. There were stables occupied by old horses that had been sent there to end their days in…well, not in peace, and one story that wouldn't have been out of place in a sketch from *Monty Python* involved a monkey escaping an experiment, before being cornered and promptly shot in the carpark behind the Seven Stiles; 'It was like King Kong takes Kent, if King Kong had been two foot tall.'

Les returned to the bar at the Seven Stiles with his brother John and he also managed to pick up a couple of shifts at a menswear shop. It was while working at the shop that Les had decided to embark on a little romance; they'd meet on the station platform in the morning and caught the same train home every night. On a snowy evening, although he can't recall quite how or why, apart from the obvious, they ended up in the woods near Les's house where a 'rather successful brief encounter transpired.'

When he wasn't tending bar at the Stiles or measuring waistlines, he would walk the streets, either looking for work or just keeping out of his mum's way. That's how it happened; one day, while making his usual inquiries shop to shop, the heavens opened and forced Les to seek shelter under a shop awning. As he waited for the shower to pass, he heard the voice that would change everything; 'Well don't just stand there, young man, come on in…'

CHAPTER TWO

Upon turning and entering, Les found himself in an army recruitment centre. Thinking nothing of it, out of politeness, he went through the motions of the enrolment procedure to bide his time until the rain eased. As the clouds broke, Les stuffed the papers into his pocket and said, without any actual intention, that he'd return them the next day. They remained in his pocket for the best part of a month until his dad was scavenging for housekeeping money. Being an ex-volunteer himself, he was over the moon and couldn't sign the papers quick enough and with that, after a while, the idea grew on Les. The more he thought about it, the better it seemed; the pay wasn't great, but it would be regular, he'd be able to travel and in doing so, he'd be getting away from his mother. He made the decision and handed in the papers.

A few weeks later, Les was summoned to join the boys service at the Junior Leaders Regiment in Oswestry. Upon arriving at

Gobowen station, army trucks were lined up and waiting. The train ride to get to Gobowen had been three hours, with the carriages almost full of new recruits, along with a couple of dozen more experienced soldiers. Training instructors from every regiment of the British Army greeted the arrivals, before they embarked on a brief journey to the barracks, where they were allocated quarters.

Once fitted in uniforms, barrack life began with the training as relentless as one would expect with endless drills; abseiling, boating, climbing Snowden and by the time a month had passed, he could march, halt, present arms, about turn, right wheel, left wheel, and could strip a rifle blindfolded.

As a new recruit, Les was exposed to a lot of intimidation, leaving him always on edge and apprehensive. Older soldiers would regularly come in and turn over the barracks, looking to pick off some lone new recruit. After a month, he was allowed to travel into town but only dressed in uniform, which he said didn't help his chances of catching the eye of a girl. Sometimes a dance would be held back at the barracks, but the majority of girls who attended would already be spoken for by the older soldiers.

At once dance in particular, Les did manage to hit it off with a local girl. Lights out was ten o'clock and he recalled being woken shortly after that by a couple of the older soldiers, who warned him that the girl he had been dancing with was spoken for, and should he proceed in his pursuit of her, they'd kick his head in. The following weekend, as Les made his way into the town, he bumped into the same girl again and told her it might not be in their best interest to take things further after the friendly warning he'd received. She burst out laughing and informed Les that the soldier in question had been unsuccessfully attempting to woo for her weeks, but she wasn't interested. Les decided to pick up where he'd left off, but after an hour of dancing in a local bar, the same soldier had tried to interrupt the dance, at which point the girl had turned to him and informed him in no uncertain terms that even if he were the last man on earth, he wouldn't be in the line of potential suitors. As satisfactory as the moment was for Les, he decided that perhaps girls, taken or otherwise, were best avoided while he was serving.

After his passing-out parade, Les was posted to St George's Barracks in Sutton Coldfield. Upon arrival he was put into barracks full of new recruits, where he had to complete his training all over again. For the first few weekends, he was once again barred from venturing into the local town in his civvies, although it mattered less now he was spending the majority of his weekends back at home.

Les was still too young to join the City of London regiment of the Royal Fusiliers so he was designated to help with the training, given he had now gone through the motions himself twice, in addition to guard duties at the front gate. He recalled a young girl that, for about a fortnight, would approach him on the gate and attempt to start a conversation. Per regulations, Les would ignore her but he remembered about a week later, while polishing his boots, the barracks descended into chaos. The armoury had been broken into and weapons had gone missing. Apparently, the young lady had found a soldier less immune to her charm on guard, and while they were in the throes of passion, her IRA sympathizer boyfriend had ransacked the armoury of its inventory.

The time arrived for Les to be sent to Germany to join his regiment; the first time he'd ever been on a plane. On arrival at Belfast Barracks in Osnabrück, he was back in the training company with all those squaddies who'd completed six weeks basic training. At this point, the war had only been over for two years and the British soldiers were still an occupying force; 'there was little love lost between us and the residents of Osnabrück.'

Despite this, you weren't too likely to actually meet many Germans who had actually fought the British because Osnabrück had been one of the major recruiting areas for the Nazis and most of them had fought the Russians. Regardless, the British were no less hated, not just for political reasons, but also on account of their soldiers' inability to handle the local beer, so even if you were allowed to pop out of an evening in your civvies, most of the local bars and restaurants wouldn't have let you in.

The First Battalion of the Royal Fusiliers was an even easier place for the bullies to operate. For many of the new recruits and younger squaddies, it was their first time abroad and so the homesickness made them even easier pickings for the older soldiers. With this in mind, a large portion of the new recruits would rarely return from their first leave, with more deserting while in Germany, either because of the bullying or the sheer monotony of the day-to-day routine. Of a morning, the duty NCO (non-commissioned officer) made his rounds by riding his bicycle through the dormitories or smashing a bin lid against someone's bed frame, usually the unfortunate soul closest to the door. If you weren't up by the time he'd done his second lap, they'd tip you out of bed, and if that ever failed, which would only usually be caused by a hangover, you'd be charged with having disobeyed orders. When Les made it to NCO, he was a little lighter handed; 'I'd just turn the lights on and tell them to get up, I wasn't their bloody mother!'

Whether it was Les or a bin lid waking you, you were expected to be dressed and have your locker clean, the contents of which required to be the appropriate folded length and ready for inspection. If anything was out of order, you'd have a second inspection in the evening, usually for the entire platoon, just to make an example of you. Obviously, it was the intention that this put a lot of pressure on all concerned, and more so if it messed up any drinking or dancing that might have been planned. Any misdemeanours would lead to loss of pay or your privileges. Punishments would vary from detention to guard duty (ideally sans IRA seductress), painting the stones of the parade ground a whiter shade of pale or kitchen duties, not to mention the endless threat of bullying.

Les said that it still shocked him to think of quite the level of intimidation, bullying and loan sharking that was rife then. The bullying was akin to the school playground, whereby anything would be taken as a sign of weakness, no matter how innocent, whether it be what team you supported, a photo of your family, etc. Unlike the forces now, where reporting of such incidents is commonplace, back then, should you inform on a bully they'd simply take a bed post to you while you slept.

Wages may have been regular, but they were low and much like life back at home, everything was bought on the tick. You could get anything you wanted to lay your hands on, but because of the soldiers being young, they had little experience with managing money and were frequently spending more than they were earning. Les managed to supplement his wages by earning a bit of extra cash babysitting, and when his dad would write to him, he'd always sent a bit of money along with the local newspaper and a couple of books.

It wasn't long before Les was selected for the NCO's cadre, and he fondly remembered when his dad came and visited for the ceremony. Arranged by the Royal Fusilier Association, Walter arrived on a coach full of fellow war veterans and they were treated to demonstrations with all the trimmings; 'I know he loved that day and he was definitely holding court in the Stiles the night he got back!'

His first duty commanding a section was to go to Norway to participate in a NATO exercise. The weather was brutal, causing the roads under their vehicles and tanks to collapse. Suddenly they came under fire (blanks), which bogged them down further. They stopped upon hearing the gunfire, abandoned their vehicle and climbed a hill to come up behind the enemy position, capturing them right away. Unfortunately for an overenthusiastic Les, the Army Marshall disallowed the strategy and they were ordered to begin the battle again.

Another exercise saw Les travel to Denmark to practice manoeuvres with the Danish army, although he said that most of the time was actually spent in the Carlsberg brewery, where the beer was tenfold stronger than that of the local brew in Osnabrück. Les reckoned the Danish had plied them with it so they wouldn't stand a chance in the morning's battles. By all accounts, as strategies went, it worked pretty well.

Whilst in Denmark, they were testing out new equipment, including an armoured personnel carrier. Les had the task of learning how to drive it as well as command it, but the only issue was that the testing ground was littered with bomb craters, so there was Les standing up in the hatch while the driver steered the vehicle down below. Inevitably they hit one of the craters, went down and then straight back up again. As the carrier hit the ground, the force tore the cable from Les's headset leaving him unable to communicate with the driver, which wasn't ideal given they were heading for another crater, this time full of water. The vehicle was written off and Les was fined.

Back at the barracks, it was evident to Les that those promoted on the last cadre had been causing a lot of jealousy and unrest among the older men, especially those who had failed where had had succeeded, and as time went on it became increasingly obvious that things were being done to undermine the young NCOs; 'Had we not been as clued up as we were, then there would have been serious repercussions, because a lot of important things were sabotaged. One fella nearly had his head taken off when this cover from an engine compartment flew off and missed him by a hairs breadth.'

The monotony of the weekends in Osnabrück were mainly broken up by drinking. Now, in the years I've known Les, he has never been a big drinker. We'd share a bottle over dinner, but he wouldn't drink in the day and I never saw him drunk nor remotely close to it, but he said that most mornings in Osnabrück you'd more often than not wake up still drunk from the night before; 'Mattresses would be so piss-soaked after weeks of the guys just going in their sleep that they'd be sagging.'

One particular incident is most likely a contributing factor to Les's reluctance to drink to excess; during a drinking game, unaware of what was actually in the concoctions being consumed, Les began to hallucinate that the army was 'out to get him', so tried to jump out of a top floor window. Fortunately, his belt snagged on the window frame, or the fall would have been fatal.

Because alcohol was so cheap, it was commonplace for soldiers to run up bar tabs that would be paid at the end of the week, something that did nothing to improve the issue of spending more than you were earning. No sooner had you been paid than your beer bill would wipe you out again.

Aside from the loan sharking and shoplifting, another disturbingly common stream of income for an indebted soldier was known as 'rolling' locals; awaiting a drunk German as he staggered from a bar and robbing him. Because in the sixties so few German's spoke English, combined with the alcohol and the poorly lit streets, it all made for any identification to be pretty difficult. Les said that it was incredibly sad to see was how easy it was for the men to be drawn into that way of life.

Les was falling behind on his payments and it started to get to him, borrowing from more and more people. He was very frank when he told me how scared he was; the people he was borrowing from, and furthermore the people he owed didn't mess around when it came to late or missed payments.

One story is still as hard for Les to tell as it is to listen to him tell it, and although he's quick to point out that the blame doesn't rest with any of those involved, it is for him the catalyst for events that would ultimately lead to him taking another man's life. Having finished preparing his uniform for the next day, Les was in the middle of his nightly routine of planning the next day's schedule and studying when he heard the casual noise from downstairs that one would expect approaching lights out. Usually that noise would quieten down fairly promptly, but on this occasion it didn't. The three men responsible for the prolonged racket were MacDermott, Renton and Commanchio, as they banged repeatedly on the door of a section commander by the name of Steadman. Les happened to know Steadman was out with a late pass, so when the noise settled down momentarily, he assumed they'd figured as much until seconds later when his own door flew open. They asked politely enough, given they were clearly intoxicated, if they could come in, to which Les obliged. They inquired as to Steadman's whereabouts, to which Les informed them honestly that he had a late pass, and they responded with a tirade of abuse against Steadman. As they grew more irate, Les offered them each a cigarette in an attempt to placate them but it definitely didn't work. Spotting his freshly pressed uniform, they set about it and the contents of his locker, trashing the room before turning their attention to Les; 'They wanted to know who the hell I thought I was trying to calm them down, and then it dawned on me they were also mad that they'd been passed over several years ago for the promotion I'd just gotten... that combined with the beer... I dread to think what would have happened if they'd been on Carlsberg instead...'

While Les had been attempting to calm the situation, he had failed to notice one of the men plugging in his steam iron. Just as he thought he'd settled the situation, or at least there was nothing left to throw around, Les still remembers his final words to them; 'See you in the morning. Do me a favour and turn the light out.'

The next thing he felt was an excruciating pain shoot through his head, emanating from his eye, then the sound of sizzling and an almighty scream. It took a moment for him to realise it was himself yelling. 'You fucking say anything to anyone, and it won't just be your fucking face that's burnt!' spat one of the attackers.

Les couldn't recall anything after that until he woke the next morning in agony and aware of 'a smell of burnt meat'. As he made his way to a mirror, he saw his face was completely bloodied and burnt, his eye engorged. Fortunately, the steam had acted as a barrier from any deep damage although two rows of holes were visible on his cheek. He managed to compose himself enough to make his way, barely dressed, to the guardroom, where he was immediately transferred to a specialist eye hospital. Tests showed there was no lasting damage and he would wear an eye-patch for several weeks while the wounds healed.

The assailants were immediately arrested and charged with grievous bodily harm and they were remanded for court martial. Unfortunately for Les, he was now portrayed as the villain in the situation, not the victim. He soon began receiving threats and many an attempt to intimidate him to not give evidence transpired. His room was regularly trashed, his belongings were all stolen, and he was shunned by anyone he'd called a friend. Word spread and soon he didn't even feel safe stepping out in town. Paranoia took hold and any confidence Les had built up in his years in the army were wiped out in one fell swoop.

Although Les had declined medical leave at the time of the incident because he didn't want his family to see his wounds, regular leave came around not long after. Although glad to see his dad, things weren't much better at home and being in a confined space with his mother was not his idea of rest bite. In hindsight, he said that he was probably close to a breakdown, had he known what one was back then.

When it was time to return to Osnabrück, Les tried to deliberately miss the train in the hope of letting the universe take care of the things, but it was not to be. As he bid farewell to his family, little did he know that he would never see some of them again – and others for fifteen years.

On a boat back, Les got struck up a conversation with another soldier he had recognised from his regiment. Unfortunately, that soldier wasted no time in telling Les what he thought of him, and his behaviour, for blowing the whistle on his attackers, and told him he hoped he got everything he deserved and more.

Les arrived back to his barracks to find his room had been destroyed; everything stripped and gone, his door kicked in, what hadn't previously been nicked had either now been stolen or had been trashed. Regaining his composure and trying to convince himself he could handle himself, he tidied his room and headed to the corporal's mess for supper only to be confronted by several of the servicemen for whom he had babysat. Each wanted to know why Les had been boasting to having slept with their wives. Quick on his feet, Les told them, on account of it being the truth, that someone was winding them up. They backed off, but that wasn't the end of it.

Les was now without belongings, his room would be trashed daily, and he was still in debt with absolutely no means of paying up as MacDermott, Renton and Commanchio did all they could to cut him off from any resources or means. Even though they were under arrest, the intimidation never stopped, and they would regularly send their foot soldiers to warn Les that his mother would be carved up if he didn't pay soon. In any other situation, Les said he would have dismissed this as nonsense, peacocking and the like, but in his fragile state of mind he said even the most innocent remark from an impartial bystander sounded like a threat.

Eventually, he couldn't cope any longer. He tortured himself with questions every day for the rest of his life; Why hadn't he asked his family for help when he was home on leave? Why did he just not get back on that train? Why didn't he take the medical leave? But he had answers for all of them the most common being he didn't want to disappoint his father.

The terrible, awful and tragic night of 3rd December 1966 that followed would change and torment the lives of so many people for a very long time…

CHAPTER THREE

On the night of 3rd December 1966, Les had gone out with the intention of stealing enough money to pay his debts. He rarely spoke privately or publicly about the incident, but I know there wasn't a day that went by that he didn't hate himself for what he had done that night. His actions would not only deprive a family of a husband and father but also destroy his own family at home; 'and furthermore a family of my own that didn't even exist yet... I've destroyed so many lives...'

Les had initially spotted a drunk man in the town who had asked him for directions, but as they walked a little together, Les found their conversation surprisingly pleasant, so felt unable to go through with his plan. He took a taxi to the barracks but said that the driver was taking a deliberately slow route, so he had asked him to pull over, insisting he would walk the rest of the way. It was at that moment that without thought, Les decided to go through with it. He pulled out a gun and demanded the driver's money, but the driver fought back, trying to get the gun from Les, and it went off. Les has always maintained he had no knowledge the gun had been loaded and would never have knowingly taken out a loaded gun, it had only ever been intended to scare the person he would rob.

Les entered the barracks by climbing over the fence to avoid being seen and returned the gun to the armoury. On doing so, he asked the store man if he realised the gun had been loaded. He replied he didn't but realising something had obviously occurred and he was by default implicated, he informed Les that should anybody make inquiries, he would say that the gun had never left. His last words to Les were, 'don't worry, it'll all blow over soon.'

Les said that his gut reaction was to hand himself in, but this was quickly quashed by an overwhelming sense that everything would actually somehow blow over soon; Maybe the driver was alright? Maybe it had never happened? And a hundred and one other ridiculous notions.

Given Les had already been in a fragile state before the shooting, his mental health suffered even more afterwards. The combination of a continuing torrent of abuse from MacDermott, Renton and Commanchio, and the guilt of what he had done were overwhelming. The armourer reassured Les continually that no one had raised any questions, only adding to his deluded line of thought that everything would wash over.

A few days later, Les was approached by a messenger and summoned to the guard room, where he was arrested and subsequently moved to Royal Military Police barracks nearby. Initially, Les denied absolutely everything but after a couple of hours, he broke down and confessed everything. Les has no memory of the interrogation itself so in the interest of impartiality, below is the statement he gave at the time.

I came back from roll call, saw Lance Corporal Norman Marks and said to him that I wanted to go out that night and asked him if he would come with me. He said 'No.' Then I said to him 'I want to go and change.' I asked him if he would give me an air pistol when I had changed.

I changed into my blue suit and check raincoat. Then I went to look for him in his room. We went together to the armoury. He suggested I should take a 9mm revolver. But I said I wanted an air pistol.

Marks pointed out that if I was going to hold somebody up with an air pistol it would be spotted right away that it was not a real gun. Then I saw the 6mm pistol and said I would take that one. The magazine was already in the gun and I asked him to wait a minute – I wanted to go and get my gloves.

Marks stayed in the armoury. I got my gloves and went back down. Marks gave me the gun and some money for a drink. After I left Marks, I jumped over the fence at the MRS. Then I went to the pub known as the Green Window. I bought a portion of chips and a beer. I spoke to Corporal Dempsey, Corporal Jasock and Corporal Reynolds.

I left the pub and went through the town, where I met this drunken German who I really wanted to rob. We went together to 10 Bremerstrasse and he asked me if I wanted to go in with him. I said 'No.' I left him and fifty to a hundred yards away I stopped a taxi.

I told the driver to take me to Albertstrasse. He drove there but stopped at Caprivi barracks. I said 'No, not here. Just go around the corner.' Then he drove round for about five minutes. He stopped in front of a house.

I pulled out the gun and asked him for money. He grabbed for the gun and at the same time tried to open the door to get out of the car. He pushed me against the door, then I heard a click. He tried to grab my hand with his right hand and open the door with his left. He was trying to open the door and pull me after him. He shrieked and screamed.

I hit him twice with the gun on the side of the neck. Then the gun went off. He started gurgling and blood flowed from his face. He let go and I let the pistol drop inside the taxi. I tried to open the door from the inside but could not. As I tried to get out of the taxi it rolled backwards. I was afraid the whole time. I pulled on the handbrake and I tried to stop the taxi. Then I pulled down the window, grabbed the door handle and opened it from outside.

I ran away up the street. But as I ran it dawned on me that I had left the pistol behind. I went back to collect it. As I opened the door his head rolled from side to side. I picked up the gun from the floor, re-loaded and heard a sudden ping. I closed the door, ran up the street and turned right. I ran to the main road and kept running until I reached the barracks. As I ran away from the taxi, I loaded the gun again. One or more bullets fell out.

As I got to the barracks, I spoke to Fusilier Abbot who was on guard at the gate. I said to him, 'You did not see me. And if anyone asks, I came back at 1 a.m.' Then I went to Marks' room, woke him and said that I wanted to see him downstairs. He got dressed and went with me to the armoury. When we got inside, I got hold of him and said, 'Did you know there were bullets in that gun?'

He said, 'Yes, why? Didn't you check?' I said 'No, I didn't think there was anything in it.'

He took the gun from me and started to clean and oil it. He cleaned it and put it away and said if anyone asked about the gun, he would say he never gave it out. Then we locked up and went upstairs, where I washed my hands. After I washed my hands, I asked what would happen if it was found out it was this gun. He said, 'I will simply say I do not know how it got out of the armoury. Anyone could get in because the lock was broken.'

Then he said to me that I should go to bed. He said he would see me the next morning and think something up. I went to bed and woke up the following morning at about nine o'clock. I saw Marks and said to him, 'Don't forget, if they find out it was me, you are also in it, because you gave me the gun and the ammunition.' He said 'Don't give me any problems, I want to get home for Christmas.'

I was sitting in the classroom when Fusilier Abbot came in and said a couple of taxi drivers came in while he was on guard duty. They were asking about another taxi driver, and the duty officer asked him if he had seen anyone come in between 1 a.m. and 3 a.m. He said he had not seen anyone. Another fusilier asked what was up. And Abbot said he would find out. Abbot then went out and the other fusilier asked me if I knew anything. I said that I knew. I also said that I was afraid and did not know what to do. Then I told him everything. He promised that he would not tell anyone. And now that I had cleaned the gun, everything would be okay. He went to eat, and I went and got a cigarette. There were then only two men in the room, Miles and Young.

Miles asked, 'Are you still going out tonight?' I said, 'No, I am in enough trouble.' I left the room and went to my room and laid on the bed. Then I searched through my locker and found there was blood on my suit and on my coat. I went back and asked Miles what he would do if I had bloodstained clothes. He told me, 'Bury them. Bring them down to the bunker.'

Then I went back to my room, laid on my bed and fell asleep. Fusilier Winters came in and asked if it would be okay with me if he could take my suit to the cleaners because he wanted to borrow it. I gave him the blue and grey mohair and said he could put it in the cleaners the following day.

The next night Marks came to me and said the SIB [the army's Special Investigations Branch] had just been and had taken the pistol. He told me to hide anything with blood on it. I went straight back to my room and cut up the suit and my coat and packed the stuff in a cardboard box. I covered everything with the News of the World.

Then I asked another fusilier if he would help me. We went together to Prestatyn barracks and found a gully. We put the stuff in and covered it with stones. I went back to the barracks and said to Marks that I had taken away the bloodstained clothes. He said, 'Good, now they won't be able to find any proof.' I said, 'Just remember who gave me the gun if they found out it was me.' He said I could rest assured that they would not find anything out from him.

That is everything apart from saying that I met the fusilier who helped me hide the clothes on Saturday, and he asked if I knew a reward had been offered. I told him I did not. I asked him if he was thinking of claiming it. He said he did not fink of anyone.

I would just like to add that at no time until the shooting did I know the gun was loaded.

Les was charged, and due to the backlash from locals, he was moved to several different British barracks around the Rhine. The State Attorney's office had put out a reward for the killer's arrest and the German authorities attempted to take over the trial and request capital punishment be restored, so heinous and coldblooded was the crime.

In every guard room or cell Les was held in, neither his name nor crime were able to be displayed on the door for fear of repercussion. He was banned from communication with any fellow prisoners and would have to request permission to have a cigarette under supervision.

Doctors and psychiatrists were sent to examine Les ahead of his trial. One in particular, he remembered asking him to identify the images he saw in ink blots; 'I told him what I saw, turned the page and so forth until I got to a blank page. When I told him it was blank, he looked at me exasperated and asked me, what on earth did I mean it was blank, couldn't I see the cottage, the lakes and the birds? He snatched the book from me and stormed out of the cell, telling the guard that I was completely off my rocker.'

Despite the Germans desperate attempt to claim jurisdiction, the case was automatically handed to British authorities. He was moved back to barracks in Osnabrück, where he was allowed slightly more freedom before a preliminary hearing that would decide whether or not there would be a case to answer. Because Les had admitted the killing, the hearing passed relatively quickly, and the case proceeded to trial at a court martial.

MacDermott, Renton and Commanchio were all either imprisoned or given dishonourable discharge while Les was awaiting his trial.

Walter and Adelaide travelled to Osnabrück, although Les was obviously much happier to see his father than his mother. He told him that although he couldn't condone what Les had done, he was with him all the way to the end.

Much like the initial interrogation, Les's memory of the trial itself is vague and passed him by in a blur. As he'd already confessed, it was a matter of listening to testimonies, evidence and other formalities. The only part that Les remembered with absolute clarity was when Felix Reese's wife took the stand; 'That's when what I'd done really, really hit home. She couldn't take her eyes off of me and I couldn't bear to look at her, I felt sick to my stomach and so ashamed.'

The man from the armoury changed his statement several times, which added to the length of the trial and various solders whom Les had never so much as passed in a corridor gave detailed witness statements and character references against him. The final person to give evidence was Les himself, who's only defence was still not knowing that the gun had been loaded. Should Les have been found guilty of intention to rob and kill a man, he would be found guilty of murder, and if only with the intention to rob regardless of whether he'd known the gun were loaded, then manslaughter. Everyone on the defence team, including his family, were quietly confident that a verdict of manslaughter would be returned, but alas it was not to be… 'life.' Les couldn't look at me when he recalled the silence that came after hearing that word.

After an emotional parting of ways with his parents, Les was returned to the guard room to await the army's automatic appeal procedure, which was quickly turned down. Arrangements were made for him to be flown from Gutersloh airport back to England, where he was to serve the rest of his life in Wormwood Scrubs.

CHAPTER FOUR

When Les arrived at Wormwood Scrubs, he was categorised as a young prisoner as he was still under twenty-one. After the standard procedure of being checked in, handing over any personal belongings, bathing and changing into his new uniform; grey trousers, navy striped shirt and tie. He was allocated prisoner number 1047 and shown to an observation cell for an initial suicide watch and interviewed over several days by a medical officer. The observation cell contained only a bed and mattress, nothing else, no chair, table, toilet; 'It was laughable when I'd just come from a military cell where I could smoke, drink, shave, piss, I had a radio and a knife and fork. Yeh, there were times when I was suicidal in prison, but that couldn't have been further from one of them.'

Les was monitored the entire time, eating, showering, shaving, going to the toilet. He'd be kept awake all night by the constant opening and closing of the observation hatch on his door.

Once the doctor had decided Les wasn't going to kill himself anytime soon, he was moved to A wing, an overcrowded Victorian building in desperate need of repair, consisting of four floors with a large portion of it sectioned of for sex offenders; 'It had that fencing separating the higher floors from the ground one so no one could jump, or worse throw someone over, but the thing was so buckled it wouldn't have stopped a mouse, let alone a man.'

Les's new cell had the luxury of a table and chair, a water jug and a wash bowl. The room measured no more than thirteen foot by seven, the walls heavily graffitied and stained with old blood, food and excrement. Due to overcrowding, it would be a few months before Les would be allowed out for recreational time, but he was put to work painting Disney figurines in the toyshop. The toyshop was manned by two prison officers and was regularly patrolled to maintain discipline, although Les said there was rarely any trouble as the majority of the young prisoners there were only serving six months or so. Les was the only young prisoner serving a life sentence.

Once a week, a lorry would come to collect the finished toys. Les's first experience of this wasn't great. The prison officer on duty had ordered Les and another worker to load the batch of toys into a barrow and to follow him to the lorry. Les rightly told him that required entering an area he wasn't allowed, but the officer ignored this and demanded he follow. As Les and the other worker hauled the barrows through the prison, Les soon noticed they were approaching the main entrance. As they passed through the inner gate, the outer gate opened, revealing the waiting lorry and... freedom.

Mayhem ensued, and the prison went into lockdown; alarms rang out, doors and gates slammed and there was a lot of yelling. Les was dragged back to his cell and was to be charged with attempting an escape.

When he was hauled before the Governor, naturally the prison officer neglected to mention Les explicitly saying he wasn't permitted to leave the toyshop. Both parties gave evidence and eventually the case was dismissed, however the prison officer would not let it go so easily; 'He got an absolute bollocking from the Governor who was obviously wise to what his game was but whenever we'd cross paths in the future he'd go out of his way to make things difficult for me, especially if it was something like a visitation and he'd make a point of the most drawn out search so I'd more often than not have no time to actually speak to whoever had come to see me.'

After a couple of months, Les, somehow undeterred by the experience, admits that he did decide that escaping prison might not be such a idea bad after all, and began to formulate a plan. With a razor, he was going to hide in the box of toys to be collected, and once the lorry had travelled a sufficient distance from the prison, he'd cut his way through the box and escape via the roof hatch. The morning of the great escape arrived and Les arrived in the workshop early. He was just about to climb into a box when a prison officer arrived and told him the lorry had broken down, and there wouldn't be a collection until the week after.

Before that could happen, Les was moved to being in charge of the stores and the hotplate, scuppering any chances of breaking out. His new job entailed distributing blankets, serving food and keeping the hotplate clean. The food was horrifically bad. Les graphically recalled the door to his cell opening at the first mealtime and the smell hitting him and his first thought was that it was the odour of the drains. The stores had its own television and on Saturday nights, Les would take it to his cell, put a blanket over the window to hide the blue light from it and plug it into his light switch to watch *Match of the Day*. Because Les was the first into the stores in the morning, he got away with this for months because he was able to return it before anyone else had noticed it was even gone.

Les recalled when he was woken in the middle of the night and told to open the stores, as another prison was on fire and its young offenders were being temporarily moved to Wormwood Scrubs; 'They were with us for a couple of months but because we were already overcrowded, you had the sex offenders and the young boys right next door to each other. Obviously those two should never meet, but like a lot of things inside back then, it was nearly impossible to enforce.'

When Les wasn't working, he'd spend a lot of his spare time reading. He'd borrow books from the stores, but his dad would also send them along with the odd dirty magazine. On one occasion, he was summoned to the Governor's office to be told he had been sent a magazine that the powers that be had deemed obscene and inappropriate; Walter had sent Les the first edition of Penthouse to feature pubic hair. Les pointed out that he'd been in the army, killed a man and was doing a life stretch and asked how much the Governor thought the magazine was actually going to corrupt him. It was, to be fair, a solid argument and needless to say Les was allowed to keep it.

After a while at Wormwood Scrubs, Les was sent to Atkinson Morley hospital in Wimbledon for brain scans; there had been a delay in his medical documents being received from the army and something relating to the attack he'd been victim to in Osnabrück had gotten the prison doctors attention.

After several scans, Les was transferred to Hammersmith Hospital, where he'd stay for several days under guard while further tests were carried out, and then suddenly, no more was said about it. Upon returning to Wormwood Scrubs, Les was informed that due to overcrowding, he would be moving to Wandsworth to be assessed for reallocation.

As there were no boys at Wandsworth, a nineteen-year-old Les found himself on a wing with adult prisoners. During his induction, Les recalled that something about his interviews and assessments were reminiscent of the time the psychiatrist had interviewed him in the guard room in Osnabrück; none of the questions made sense and he got the distinct feeling they were trying to catch him out or make him question his own sanity.

At Wandsworth, Les was sent to work in the mailbag shop, stamping the post office logo onto those old blue mail bags, which unsurprisingly, he described as incredibly tedious; 'It wasn't as bad as I'd feared, and we did have a laugh there, more than I'd had in the stores at the Scrubs. We'd muck about sewing up people's trouser legs or the arms on their jackets before their visits for a laugh. I didn't have much reading matter to pass the time as my mail wasn't being forwarded yet, so I wasn't getting anything my dad was sending, instead I kept getting some other Grantham's mail which I had to keep returning to the mailroom.'

Once his assessment was completed, Les was told he was to be moved to Albany Prison on the Isle of Wight, then regarded as the toughest maximum-security prison in the country. Having heard his mail to his son wasn't being passed on, Walter visited Les and was shocked to hear where he was being moved to the very next day.

After breakfast, Les was packing when he was summoned to the Governor's office and within several hours, found himself back in Wormwood Scrubs; a furious Walter had phoned his local MP, who was a junior minister at the Home Office, who had in turn phoned an executive in the prison service, who had informed the MP that not only was Les not being transferred to Albany, but nor had he ever been in Wandsworth and was in fact in Wormwood Scrubs, where he'd been the whole time; 'the inmate I'd been receiving mail for was down for Wandsworth and they'd mistakenly moved me instead, which explained everything, including why that doctor had looked at me as if I were completely stark raving mad in the assessment... a world class prison system in action there.'

Les saw the state of Wormwood Scrubs in a whole new light upon his return; none of the prisoners from Wandsworth would have put up with the condition of the place. Everything from the cells to the food to the toilet facilities. Wormwood Scrubs didn't even have shower facilities and the only hot water was in the kitchen. Far over capacity, the Victorian plumbing just couldn't cope; 'when they opened the water tanks in the roof, there were more dead pigeons in them than there was water. If Basil Fawlty had run a prison, it would have been Wormwood Scrubs.'

It was eventually decided the wing would be overhauled; 'Obviously in the real world, this would take years using skilled labourers, but no one was going to cough up for that, so you can guess who had to do it ourselves.'

Although it was a botch job, Les insists the end product wasn't too shabby, but with up to three prisoners sharing a cell for up to fifteen hours a day and a bucket between them, it didn't take long for it to fall back into its former state. Fortunately, Les had worked out his own system of getting into the stores early, to use the large sinks and their hot water to have a proper wash.

The mesh fence preventing jumpers was replaced with a canopy which also provided the hotplate with protection from pigeon faeces; 'the loft floors were literally knee deep in pigeon shit, so they'd send the borstal boys up there to clear it out because they were only teenagers, so no one really cared about health ramifications or anything like that. I was just glad we didn't have any bloody chimneys!'

After two years of incarceration, Les turned twenty-one and in 1968, was moved to D wing, where the long-term adult prisoners were kept. On the morning of his move, he was kept in his cell until everybody had gone about their business. Some items such as his pot and utensils had to be handed in, as he'd later be issued with new ones. He was given a brief fitting for a new uniform and a quick medical check-up before his young prisoner cell card was replaced with a new one, his new adult prisoner number was 261006. He was given his new pillowcase, sheets, socks and utensils and waited at the gate with several other prisoners awaiting transfers.

One he was escorted into D wing, the landing officer told him to report to the medical office for another examination. Les's protest that he'd already been through it in the boys' wing was ignored and he was sent down to the medical officer's room where he answered the same set of questions once more before being send back up to the landing officer and led to his new cell.

Les had arrived just in time for lunch, where it was procedure to be assigned a table. In D wing, you had the option to eat at a table or in your cell, although Les said the prison officers were always suspicious of anyone that chose to eat in their cell, thus spending more time essentially locked up than necessary. After an initial probation period, prisoners also had the option to request to eat in the recreation area, where a film would be shown once a week; 'There was also a tiny little stage in there too and they'd put shows on for us, we saw some wonderful people; David Frost, Jet Harris, Rod Stewart. I remember a girl called Kathy Kirby coming and singing for us and when she'd finished, she took a bow and the guys went mad, because they could see right down her dress because it was so low cut. For that, she got a better applause than when they had Johnny Cash go into Folsom Prison!'

From the men at his canteen table, Les was given a crash course in how things ran on the long-term wing. A recent spate of cases of blindness and a couple of deaths had occurred as a result of inmates brewing their own booze from wood alcohol and pineapple juice, but on the upside the pay was higher than it had been in the boy's wing although you didn't receive actual cash, it was all logged against the prisoners name in a register and upon release they'd be given anything you had left over. The homemade alcohol was being stored in the fire extinguishers; 'Fuck knows what would have happened if there'd been an actual fire!'

Tobacco was smuggled in by the staff and was like cash, and cash was of course king. Les later found out that one guard had even retired to the South of Spain on the successful proceeds of his illicit smuggling activities. In subsequent years, the arrival of both the Great Train Robbers and the Krays associates only led to an increase in such dealings.

Les was assigned to the mattress shop for work, picking out the horsehair filling from the used mattresses and preparing them to be refilled after the cases had been laundered; 'Years later, when the wing was refurbished, they replaced all the horsehair ones with foam ones and the first thing the sex offenders did was cut curiously positioned holes in them.'

Prisoners in for crimes against children were, among other things, regularly scalded with hot water, but some were smart and got in with the gangs, pointing out innocent prisoners as being perpetrators of their own crimes to deflect any unwanted punishment or attention, but some guards were known for taking justice into their own hands and circulating prisoners case history to some of the more notorious inmates.

Les fondly recalled one particular evening, when the prison drama group was performing a play about two men in love with the same woman; 'There was a scene where one of the men was so intimidated by the audience, when it came to deliver his line, he was just awful and the whole room was laughing. I muttered, I thought under my breath, 'I could do better than that' and from nowhere, this man behind me leans forward. Now he looked like a poor man's Quentin Crisp, with this great big bouffant hair and a scarf you'd have probably asked to borrow. Anyway, he leans in and he says to me, 'Well if you think you can do better young man, join the drama group."

The next day, Les applied, and the very next day after that, he was turned down, as there were no vacancies, but he was invited to join the stage management team, which he gladly accepted. At the same time, he was also promoted from the mattress shop to the library, where he organised books and would cut the corners of all the paperbacks returned by prisoners where their name and number had previously been. Anything in need of some maintenance was sent to the bookbinding shop where it would be furnished with a hardback cover and resold in a local shop, the proceeds from which went to funding the drama group.

On Les's first night in stage management, he met the actors and the director, Jon Haerem. Although Les had turned up with the intention of making tea, Jon told him they were short on numbers and he'd need to help read. The next day at rehearsal, he was told as the lead actor was off having some unexpected electric shock therapy, they were even further down on numbers and so Les would be playing the role of 'Tommy'; 'The story went that this guy was off having shock therapy and they'd show him pictures of boy scouts and if he responded, they'd zap him. How true that is I don't know but it didn't seem to affect his acting. Read into that what you will.'

In no time at all, Les had a couple of plays under his belt, instantly taken with the drama group. He was a natural, even catching the attention of a couple of agents, to which his response was always 'I'll give you a call in 1990!'

He fondly recalled meeting Pamela Salem, someone he spoke of often, who'd go on to be a lifelong friend; 'She was brought in to replace a much older actress in a play called *The Anniversary* but try as they might, they weren't able to age this beautiful creature.'

Les was also asked to join the prisoners union, which successfully managed to campaign for extra visits and luxuries including some new televisions; 'Until then, there were only two televisions, one at either end of the wing. The ones who ran the wing had the front row and the rest of the seats would be reserved with towels. It looked like a Spanish seaside resort at sunrise, which was funny considering we didn't have a single German on the wing.'

The success of the union was short-lived, spoiled by the arrival of Walter 'Angelface' Probyn, who'd been moved from Durham Prison after he'd broken both his ankles in a failed bid to escape. He tore apart the union as soon as he'd gotten himself elected into it and then set about making changes in the prison, with the intention of turning it into a much more relaxed affair.

One evening, when the atmosphere was particularly strained, Freddie Foreman instructed Les and several others to lock themselves in their cells. The time came for the remaining prisoners to be locked up for the night and they refused, barricading the doors to the wing in an albeit peaceful protest. When the situation was diffused, Probyn had vanished, only to be discovered the next morning in the Governor's office, where he'd destroyed his own records. Shortly after his release, Probyn was returned to prison for child molestation, which Les found curious on account of him always having had a reputation inside for violence against rapists or molesters.

Although two prisoners failed to return from home leave and one fled from the hospital in the dead of night, no one actually managed to successfully escape during Les's time at Scrubs, though he was indirectly responsible for one failed attempt. Les had been working in the tailor shop, unpicking and remaking socks, when one day he'd bumped into an old school mate. As they caught up, Les failed to concentrate on the job in hand, not realizing that he'd now sewn a twenty-foot-long sock. He ripped it from the frame, went to the toilet and stuffed it up his shirt to avoid punishment. After bidding farewell to his friend, he took a detour to the exercise yard where he discreetly removed the sock and kicked it over the wall. Within ten minutes, the wing was put on lockdown, angering everyone as teatime was subsequently delayed by over an hour; 'This woman had been out walking her dog when all of a sudden she saw this great big long sock come over the fence and thinking someone was escaping, telephoned the police.'

It was around this time when, resigned to be a lifer, Les became suicidal and resolved to hang himself. He gave his belongings to the prisoner in the cell next door under the pretence he needed to clean, closed his door and stood on his chair; 'I was about to put my tie around my neck when I thought I might need it for my next visit. In that moment, I just started laughing, slipped, fell off the chair and knocked myself out. Now luckily, I hadn't tied the tie, or I'd have hanged myself there and then. I came round, collected my belongings and just got on with it.'

Les was serving alongside some heavyweight villains. Freddie Foreman, Frank O'Connell and Buster Edwards all had their place at the top table, but Freddie warning Les to lock himself up during Probyn's failed escape wasn't the only time the gangster had his back; Frank O'Connell and Les would rip floorboards out together during the wings refurbishment and had one day gotten into a fight when Frank took offence to Les talking to an officer from the boys' wing of the toyshop. After being separated by guards, it was apparent to Les that Frank wasn't going to let go of whatever the issue was. Freddie later approached Les and asked what his problem was with Frank. The next day Frank apologised to Les and the matter was promptly put to bed.

Les and Frank worked together for another week before Les was allocated to Tom, another gentleman whom Les often spoke of with great affection. Les stayed with Tom until he left the prison service to set up a painting and decorating business that Les would later work for, upon his release.

Gangsters aside, Les also recalled the day he encountered true evil; 'I was called to reception one day, and as I was approaching the door of the officer I'd been called to see, there were several other prisoners sat on chairs, waiting to be seen. None of them particularly stood out at all, save for one. There was just something off about him, I couldn't explain it. I had this ice-cold feeling rush through my entire body, like when you get butterflies but really unpleasant, it was a horrible feeling. The hairs on the back of my neck stood up and I felt my knee's almost buckle. I swallowed hard and kept walking, trying to keep my composure. Later in the day, I was told it was Ian Brady.'

After Tom had left, Les applied for a job in the education department, cleaning the rooms before classes and making tea. He was well liked there, on account of them already being familiar with him from his presence in the drama group. Initially only an evening job, the department was soon expanded to include A-Levels and O-Levels; 'I had to make tea for the new teachers coming in for interviews and remember this one woman had to sit on the floor because there weren't enough chairs. It must have been summer because she had a very floaty, loose dress on. I walked in and I swear to god she had no knickers on, I could see everything! They must have had very high hiring standards because apparently it wasn't enough to get her the job.'

Another female teacher would also stick in Les's mind; after class, he was pulled aside and informed by her that she had a crush on him. Once he'd gotten over the shock, they embarked on a secret love affair, stealing any moments they could in cleaning cupboards and classrooms.

While working in the education department, Les's appeal was briefly reopened when two prisoners who'd shared a cell with the main witness in his case came forward with new information. However, Kenneth Nelson, the star witness in question, couldn't be found as he was moving about a lot with work, so the appeal was adjourned. When he was eventually found in October 1969, Les's case was heard at the Old Bailey, this time with a different judge as the original one was dealing with the Krays appeal. The case was promptly dismissed after the Army's QC and the judge spoke privately, but Les wasn't privy to the reason why.

Upon returning, he was told he'd be moving to a domestic offenders' wing of Portsmouth Kingston Prison, which he was disappointed to hear, especially given a lot of people had been confident he was going to win his appeal. Until the new appeal had presented itself, he'd adjusted to prison life. He was comfortable in the drama group and had even taken up writing plays, several of which had been performed and well received. He was content enough with work, keeping his head down and getting on with things as best he could, though life was no doubt more tolerable with the love of a good woman. After a brief, but intimate farewell in which his teacher-turned-lover promised to visit him, Les was put on a bus to begin the next chapter of his sentence.

CHAPTER FIVE

Les wasn't as well received as he'd hoped he would be at Portsmouth, by neither prisoners or staff; 'These were people that had killed men, women, children, and they thought I was shit on their shoes. It was a very relaxed atmosphere there and they were convinced I was going to change all that.'

Portsmouth was indeed more relaxed. Outside groups were brought in for football, as well as the drama group, which Les was asked to join, albeit at a supporting role level, which gave him more time to concentrate on his writing.

The only real work at Portsmouth was in the electric shop, where they'd assemble dimmer switches. Shortly after his arrival, the prison psychiatrist introduced himself to Les and attempted to explain how the assembly line was part of his own unique brand of therapy. Naturally, Les responded by telling him that he was as mad as his patients and went on strike, locking himself in his cell and refusing to come out. After negotiating with the Governor, Les was moved to the education block, where he was in assigned a job working in coordination with a local college writing learning aids.

A play he'd written was being performed at Wormwood Scrubs, so he was granted permission to travel back there to watch it. He stayed for several days and was able to borrow a typewriter from the education department and begin work on another masterpiece. When he returned to Portsmouth, he applied to borrow another but was refused. After several months, he applied to study a playwriting course, forcing the prison to provide him with one.

He'd write to television networks asking if they could send him scripts to study and would then watch television in the education block, trying to differentiate between normal scripts and camera scripts. He would also write poetry, and passed his writing course with flying colours.

Les was then assigned a new English teacher, with whom the conversation promptly turned to sex. He'd write her poems with hidden, suggestive meanings and she'd visit him once a week. Initially Les was indecisive as to whether his feelings were reciprocated but those thoughts were quickly quelled when she turned up to a lesson with nothing but a raincoat, and another inevitable love affair began.

Les was lucky, as not all prisoners were as fortunate when it came to the relief of tension; 'If you ever wanted to know if it's possible to be put off Penthouse magazine, one day I walked into the communal showers and had the misfortune to bear witness to one prisoner shagging the arse off another with a centrefold quite literally stapled to his back.'

Homosexual activity has, for perhaps obvious reasons, always been rife within the prison system and Les dodged his fair share of romantic interludes.

Les accepted the much-coveted job of a baker, a job there were two perks to; the first was that although you were the first up and in, once breakfast was out the way, you had the remainder of the day to yourself, which blessed Les with the time to write. The second was that during Les's employment, there was a national bread strike, creating a moral dilemma; do the prisoners strike with the rest of the country or continue to break bread while the country goes without? After some tense negotiations, it was decided that the prison kitchen would purchase extra ingredients and manufacture additional bread for the prison staff. As well as the inevitable and subtle under-the-table tobacco exchanges, at the end of the strike, donations from the staff were distributed among the workers personal bank accounts, to be redeemed upon their release.

Les once again thrived in the drama group, as they slowly began to appreciate his natural talent. He was given the responsibility of being in charge of entertainment and liaised for local actors to come in and perform alongside the prisoners.

One evening, Les had been in his cell running lines for the next night's performance when none other than the prison psychiatrist knocked on his door; 'I told him he was lucky he'd caught me in, but it went over his head.'

The psychiatrist led Les to the dining room where he introduced him to a prisoner by the name of Bruno. Bruno had been captured by the police in the midst of running amuck in the streets brandishing a carving knife, while trying to locate his wife and the young gentleman he'd discovered she was having an affair with. The psychiatrist had a theory that someone who'd actually killed someone would be the best person to convince Bruno why murder wasn't the answer. Les reeled off the usual, and obvious reasons, why stabbing the illicit lovers to death wasn't the best course of action, but with every hour that passed, Bruno only became more agitated, angry and determined. As the sun came up, Les took one look at the prison psychiatrist, then turned to Bruno and told him 'fuck it, do it, kill them, I don't give a toss!'

With that, Bruno collapsed in tears, declaring his undying love for his wife. Les wished Bruno luck and told the psychiatrist he'd see himself home, which also went completely over his head.

Unfortunately, even being called upon for such emergencies, teamed with his keep-your-head-down-and-get-on-with-it attitude to work, and good standing in the drama group, made little difference to his parole application, turned down on Christmas Eve with the addendum that he wasn't permitted to apply again for another seven years. Considering one prisoner who'd murdered four people received parole upon his first application, and another whom had skinned his wife alive was about to be released, the seven-year embargo was as good as unheard of.

On Christmas Day, the officer in charge of the sick bay called on Les and permitted him to call his parents. He offered him a little bit of Irish in his coffee and then told him he had to show him something, but Les wouldn't be able to say he'd seen it; it was a report, signed by the psychiatrist, stating that Les was a danger to himself and others, and thus should not be released.

The Governor had petitioned the Home Office regarding the parole decision, but it wasn't them that had declined the request, it had been the Army, who's jurisdiction Les still fell under, determined to make a continued example of him. All the prison staff had signed the petition in Les's favour, with exception of the psychiatrist.

A couple of days after Christmas, Les was summoned to the Governor's office and informed that he would once again be moving prisons, but this time to Leyhill. Les couldn't believe it upon first hearing; Leyhill was an open prison, occupied by either non-violent prisoners or inmates finishing out the last of their sentences.

The day of his departure, Les found out that the move had been at the behest of the prison officers for whom Les had made the bread for during the strike. After saying his farewells, he made his way toward the gate where he would encounter none other than the psychiatrist who'd come down to wish him luck. Les shook his hand, leaned in and muttered simply, under his breath; 'Cunt.'

CHAPTER SIX

HMP Leyhill was a lot like the barracks of Oswestry, row after row of huts, each housing three or four prisoners in individual rooms. Unlike Portsmouth or Wormwood Scrubs, there were no high fences or imposing metal gates. The windows didn't have bars and the doors were only locked by the inmates themselves should they wish to. Prisoners would regularly leave for group excursions and external activities. There were football and rugby pitches, a cricket field, a bowling green and a church; the latter was popular as it allowed your family to come with you, thus an extra visit.

Upon arrival, prisoners were first put to task in the garden so they could be observed, and it be determined what kind of work they'd be suitable for; Les was sent to the kitchen where he was expected to live up to his reputation as a master baker.

At 5 a.m., they'd prepare the bread for the day, desserts for lunch and desserts for dinner and then the day was his own, usually to sunbathe, weather-permitting. Les quickly worked his way up to number one in the kitchen, and also helped in the officers' club and prison officers' children's playgroup.

Les joined the drama group, reuniting him with several friends from Portsmouth and Wormwood Scrubs. Unlike the two previous prisons, Leyhill allowed local residents to come in as a paying audience; the money from ticket sales went into the prisoners committee main fund. Then, each time they wanted to put on another play, they would have to put in an application for the money from the funds to do so.

Every group at Leyhill had a committee and a respective council member who'd attend council meetings, where the council chairman and his fellow counsellors would determine the fate of just about everything.

Les was reluctantly elected as the drama groups committee member, but soon took a more active interest when he realised that the fund was being taken advantage of by prisoners. The drama group was by far the biggest contributor to the fund, but prisoners from other groups had been using it to purchase luxuries, including two new television sets.

Now Les wasn't going to grass, but he was going to make sure the drama group got what they were entitled to. As the person who was in charge of negotiating with the hire companies, he'd become aware that savings could be made. Certain items were cheaper to buy outright than to be rented a couple of times a year. He made the relevant application to the council and it was immediately turned down with a vote of no confidence; 'When the next round of elections came about, I got myself voted onto the council. My first order of business was to approve the purchase of the lamps I'd wanted from the hire company for the drama group and then I resigned. I might have been tempted to try and hang myself again if I'd had to sit through one more meeting listening to T. Dan Smith, adoring the sound of his own voice.'

The liaison officer for the drama group, John Shergold, suggested that Les join the literary society so he'd be able to go on day trips to see outside productions; there were three visits a year to either the Bristol Old Vic or The Theatre Royal in Bath. Like any group trips, the list of willing participants was lengthy, the winners obviously determined by the chairman of each group. Until John Shergold was promoted to chairman of the drama group, it had never actually been actors that had gotten to go on the theatre trip. It was one of the most popular trips as the interval of the plays meant you could have a beer; 'I'm pretty sure he knew half the group was missing, but he didn't mind so long as the half he could see were really into the play and the other half were there in time for the minibus to leave.'

Friends or family of prisoners that lived near the theatres would come and see the plays with them. One prisoner who owned a couple of clubs went one further and would go to one of his establishments while the play was on and spend the afternoon with his girlfriend.

Les only skived off once, almost unintentionally. The theatre bar was closed so he and a couple of others had decided to visit the pub over the road. They walked in to find three of Leyhill's prison officers drinking at the bar. When they were questioned why they were there, Les, quick as a flash, told them that the theatre bar had been closed, so Shergold had sent them over to see if this one was any good, but presumably not, if they were drinking there; 'Not only did they buy the excuse, but they also bought a round for us! I made an excuse about the others presumably having found a better pub, so we could scarper before they sussed what was going on.'

Les's first theatre trip was a surreal and enlightening affair. His brother Philip had sent him some clothes to wear, yet he was still convinced that the general public would know he was a prisoner. When they arrived outside the theatre, stepping off that minibus was the first time Les had set foot in public in seven years. He narrowly avoided being hit by a car, having forgotten what traffic even was. In the theatre, watching *The Duchess of Malfi*, surrounded by that huge audience, it was the first time he'd seen so many people in one place outside of a classroom or prison wing. It was so mesmerizing that he remembered nothing of the play itself. When the interval came, John Shergold bought them all a drink. Stood there in the bar, surrounded by people, out there in the big wide world, Les was overwhelmed with grief at the realisation he'd, by his own hand, lost his youth and missed out on so much.

Upon returning, the prisoners changed back into their uniforms and returned to their huts to unload their newly acquired contraband. Les was paid half an ounce of tobacco every time he cleaned the officers club, so had a decent supply of it to sell at an inflated price in times of high demand. This meant he had cash to spend on shopping trips and any luxuries, pending approval from the Governor; 'It wasn't as bad as an open prison, but you put rules in place anywhere and there'll be someone that has to break them.'

When Les had begun working in the kitchen, the staff had been allowed extras, but most would abuse the system and sell it on to the other prisoners. That had a knock-on effect, as more was being dealt under the table than over it, so extras were banned, and rations implemented.

Some of the prisoners had dietary restrictions, be it for health or religious reasons. One in particular, Sandhu, was supposed to be on a meat-free diet, which in prison consisted of little more than a piece of fruit, a bit of cheese and an omelette. He'd offered to prepare his own meals, but that request was denied. One day, Sandhu appeared before Les with nothing but a bit of solitary bit of cheese and bread on his plate. Les gave him a yoghurt and some extra fruit and then set about negotiating with the Governor for welfare officers from the Sikh and Hindu community to come into the prison and work with the kitchen on a menu that catered for all of the inmates' needs.

Les's family were visiting regularly, but whenever Walter would come alone, Les would ask him not to bring his mother anymore, as he could tell it was putting a strain on their already-deteriorated relationship. His sister Angela would write regularly as well as coming down with her husband Graham. Les's brother was working in Bristol and would write but rarely visited, as he was still trying to conceal his homosexuality from his family at the time.

Aileen Bescoby, the new welfare officer, was in charge of resettlement. Les's first assignment saw him paired with a fellow prisoner, Danny, and the two ventured into Wotton-under-Edge to garden for an old lady; 'Resettlement was just another term for slave labour, that was my summation of the whole thing.'

Resettlement work wasn't supervised, but obviously the people the prisoners worked for were quick enough to report any bad behaviour. Danny ended up being reassigned to a new job after the old woman they were gardening for reported him for constantly wondering off to make calls from the payphone at the end of the street.

At the end of one shift, Les met Jay, a new resettlement officer and was immediately smitten with her, but in a way, he says that felt more meaningful than his previous trysts. At Leyhill, he'd have to pass her office most mornings and would go out of his way to pass it on the mornings he didn't, always exchanging glances.

Being connected to a couple of well-known actors, Aileen Bescoby had elected that Les was going to be her new pet project. She told Les that she knew a couple of actors from the Old Vic who would come and stay with her whenever they visited Bristol, and although a meeting with them never came to fruition, Les did credit her with having introduced him to Louise Jamieson.

She also decided she was to take him shopping; 'I knew there wasn't any point in saying no, because she'd made her mind up, so I thought I may as well go along with it, because I needed my barnet doing.'

That weekend had been open day at the prison and someone had taken a photograph of Les in which he looked dishevelled and skeletal; 'To give you an idea of how bad I looked, it was the photo the press leapt on to publish when my crime was revealed. When I saw the state of myself, I couldn't help but wonder what on earth this woman saw in me, but then who knows what goes on in the mind of a woman? Certainly not you or me!'

The shopping trip was odd and hurried. Les had been determined to pick out a new pair of shoes, jeans, perhaps a shirt but instead he was rushed into buying a jacket he had little affection for so Bescoby could call into her flat on the way back to the prison to pick up something important. There, she made Les a cup of tea and vanished before reappearing ready to ravish him; 'You should have seen the state of it, stockings cutting into her thighs, the worst bra you ever saw, she looked a fright! A weaker man might have been turned by the experience!'

'I think it's time we were getting back', Les told her.

And so, after a frosty car ride back to the prison, during which every time Les attempted to make small talk, Bescoby would gently yet passive-aggressively turn up the radio, Les was dumped at the prison reception.

The next day, as Les made his way across the carpark in front of the officers' club, he was forced to leap out of the way of a car that drove straight toward him. It missed him by inches, veering off of the tarmac and onto the lawn, where it finally halted. Les watched as the vehicle reversed and parked neatly, before a completely calm Bescoby emerged from it and walked inside the prison like nothing had happened; 'If I hadn't seen the mad old cow coming for me, there's no way I'd have gotten out the way in time.'

Jay called Les into her office to ask how the shopping trip had gone. He didn't mention the attempted romantic interlude but asked if she'd be good enough to return the jacket for him without mentioning it to Bescoby. As he left her office, Bescoby collared him, angrily demanding to know what he and Jay had been talking about, to which he calmly replied 'resettlement'.

The next week, Bescoby took sick leave and never returned. Les later found out she had been diagnosed with leukaemia and died a short while after.

Les was asked if he'd like to submit a play he had written, *A Reason to Live*, not so subtly about unrequited love, in which a dying woman is revisited from people from her past, to the Gloucester one-act-play festival. After a few alterations, it was entered into the category for Best Original Play. Though Les insists the competition was fierce, *A Reason to Live* was accepted and the drama group was invited to perform it as Leyhill Amateur Dramatic Society.

On the day of the festival, the sets that had been lovingly crafted were loaded onto a truck and the drama group climbed aboard their minibus. As they were about to set off, they were informed that no one from the prison was willing to escort them and because of this, there was no one to drive the truck. Shergold and Jay both showed up but neither had the appropriate licence to drive it. After some negotiating, it was decided that they only really needed a chair, which was loaded into the back of the minibus. Shergold elected himself to be the escort while Jay drove; 'She was a great girl, gave us a lot of time. She was always being pulled in a hundred and one directions at that place, but she'd always be there watching rehearsals and she didn't have to, bless her.'

The play being performed before *A Reason to Live* also had a minimalistic set, so not too much work was required prepping the stage. Les said the woman who played the lead was marvellous. While they awaited a decision from the judges, Les got talking to a gentleman who worked for the theatre and told him that they'd recently been awarded a grant and were about to undergo a refurbishment. When he heard all of their seats would be scrapped, Les spotted the opportunity to do a deal and offered to buy them. Leyhill's seats at the time were standard steel and plywood, whereas Gloucester's were luxurious, green velvet lined. The gentleman said he wasn't allowed to sell them, but if Leyhill were able to make a donation to the theatre, they were welcome to take them off his hands.

After returning to Leyhill with his play having won first prize, Les applied to the council for £25 to be donated to Gloucester Theatre for the seats. At the time, the drama group was handing all of its money into the main fund, so by default, it was technically funding every new purchase within the prison. With this in mind, a frustrated Les went straight to Shergold and told him what was going on. Shergold threatened to suspend the council if the purchase order wasn't pushed through immediately and within a fortnight, the drama group were fitting their new seats.

A few months later, it was Jay's time to move on and she announced she was leaving the prison. She told Les she'd be calling in from time to time and hoped they could stay in touch, asking if she could write to him. He gave her the name of someone on his visitors list that no longer came to see him, and good on her word, wrote to him regularly.

Bill in the kitchen had also moved on to pastures new and a new kitchen officer arrived. He was from Dartmoor and couldn't have been more different from Bill; 'He was one of those fellas that was obsessed with the rules, reciting them like Dot Cotton quotes the bible.'

It was only a matter of time before he and Les clashed, when the kitchen officer demanded Les be removed from the drama group as he didn't think such a thing instilled the appropriate discipline or was suitable punishment for someone who had committed such a crime. He even had the backing of several officers, who also had it in in for him, even though their wives, quite taken with him, unsuccessfully petitioned for Les to remain in the drama group. This left the relationship fraught between Les and the kitchen officer, so he quit and applied for a new labour position.

He was assigned to the library where his new job entailed vetting the Leyhill News, a condensed weekly paper printed on a single side of A4 paper. It would contain brief reviews of shows, minutes of council meetings, prison letters and cartoons. It was ultimately the Chief who had final say as to what went in, but it was down to Les to submit to him what he thought should be included.

An influx of letters from prisoners regarding the state of the kitchen and decline of its services brought Les's attention to his replacement who was at odds with the new kitchen officer as he attempted to run things the old way; 'In hindsight, he'd probably rather have kept me on because the guy that replaced me was up to no good from the minute he got the job, selling food under the table, extra portions going missing here, there and everywhere.'

Moussa, an Indian inmate who Les had been pals with, also confided in him that he was stressed over the food situation and so with the approval of the Chief, some of the letters were printed in the Leyhill News. Needless to say, the next time Les was in line for his supper, the portion was less than adequate and when he questioned this, Les was sentenced to seven days in a closed jail in Gloucester. He had a visit scheduled later that afternoon which he requested be cancelled, but it was inevitably not. Two days into the sentence, a couple of officers arrived from Leyhill to take him back and the kitchen worker had been suspended for the grief caused.

Les returned to duties at the library but no longer as editor. He was largely left to his own devices and the library officer would take him into town whenever Les needed to pick up props for plays.

They'd always stop by a little restaurant on the way, just outside of Bristol and after becoming friendly, when that library officer took over the drama group, his first order of business was re-instating Les.

Shortly after that, Les was spotted by the head of Bristol Old Vic while performing and was offered a summer school place, though the Home Office rejected the idea immediately. However, he was allowed to accept a place at Filton College, taking courses in English Literature and Film Studies; 'No complaints from me. They turned me down for the Old Vic, because they thought it would be full of women, which it wasn't, yet they approved a college packed with them!'

Per usual, it wasn't just college where Les had his head turned. At Leyhill, he had also joined the art group, recommended to him by a fellow inmate and gifted painter, Derek, on account of its regular trips, and Les had in turn introduced him to the drama group for the same reason. The teacher was an added attraction to the group for Les. One day she had brought in a series of photographs of herself. Les was privy to seeing one that for some reason evaded the rest of the group, a photo taken by her ex, in which she was completely naked. After class, he asked her if she'd like to have a drink with him one day after college and she agreed. The next week as planned, he made his excuses and escaped the library to meet her in a pub next door. After a few drinks, they went for a walk, which was followed by sex on Clifton Downs. But it wasn't meant to be, and when drama classes resumed after their summer hiatus, Les quit the art class.

On another prison open day, Les and Derek were chatted up by two female visitors in their thirties, and they arranged to meet them after college. Les would give the college library the usual slip and together, the four of them would drive to Tintern Abbey for regular trysts.

For Les, all of these women, by his own admission, were nothing more than sex. He had the woman he was in love with always in his mind, and although they would write to each other regularly, he never told her how he felt for fear of scaring her off, and of course the fact that several years remained before he was even eligible for parole.

Derek moved on in December, leaving Les largely alone in terms of close friends. That Christmas, the new watch he was gifted by Walter was stolen and so the festive season was spent steeped in depression as he attempted to uncover the culprit. No one appeared to have seen anything, though two people, a night patrolman and a Welsh inmate, appeared to show a suspicious amount of concern for Les's plight.

Just when he thought he'd given up any hope of getting it back, word reached him that someone was attempting to sell a watch. Les set up a meeting and lay in wait in the greenhouse, determined to ambush the person, when he heard his name called by two prison officers; the Welshman had been found in possession of the watch as well as several other stolen items. The watch was returned to Les and the Welshman moved to another prison, for fear of retribution from the others he'd also been stealing from.

One particular event, though trivial at the time, would leave a mark on Les. His Indian friend Sandhu approached him one day in the cafeteria and asked him if he'd look after something for him; a string of beads, to be kept with him in his left pocket, for ten days. For those ten days, Les didn't see Sandhu, but when he reappeared to collect the beads, he handed Les a piece of paper with the number '27378' written on it. He said nothing but gave Les a knowing nod and thanked him.

Later that day, Les was summoned to see the assistant governor who told him his sentence had been overruled by the Army and he was to be transferred to a hostel scheme at Wormwood Scrubs the very next day; 'That night the officers all gave me their idea of a send-off by soaking me with fire buckets and locking me out of my room. Eventually I managed to get back into it to find everything gone but my mattress, but it didn't really matter as I couldn't sleep anyway, I was so excited to be getting out of that place.'

CHAPTER SEVEN

It was 1977 when Les boarded the bus from Leyhill with £17.11p in his pocket; 'I remember looking down to see if anyone had dropped anything for the prisoners as they used to do and then it dawned on me it was now my turn, so I stuck five quid in a cigarette packet and put it by the curb.'

At Temple Meads Station, completely bewildered, Les showed his travel warrant to the ticket officer, who directed him to the correct platform and wished him luck; 'I wondered what he meant at first, then realised he must have seen so many prisoners going through on the same route... or maybe he just thought I looked like I needed luck!'

While waiting for his train, Les went into the newsagents to buy some stationary, excited at the prospect of corresponding on paper that didn't have Leyhill Prison's address stamped across it.

Sat in the smoking carriage, it was the first time Les had been on a train in over a decade. He wrote letters to a few friends with news that he was out and would be contactable at his parents. Then he sat back, lit a cigarette and took in the scenery as the train made its way to Cove.

After asking several people for directions, he found himself on a vast estate of identical houses, and sometime later, eventually rang the doorbell of the correct one. Walter had offered to take the day off work to be home to greet him, but Les had insisted he'd see him when he got in from work. Instead, the door was answered by his mother, who silently ushered him in. Les recalled the house being cluttered and untidy, commenting that, despite it only being the two of them living there and Walter being at work all day, housework didn't appear to be high on her agenda. Les fixed them both a cup of tea and then listened to his mother talk about the neighbours, the old house, Walter, John… anything to avoid asking how he was, how his journey had been, how it felt to be out or how it felt to be home.

After making the bed up in his new room he said was no bigger than his cell, he set about cleaning the house; 'The more you cleaned, the more you found to clean. I vacuumed the whole place from top to bottom, dusted, cleaned the kitchen, cleaned out the bath, bleached the toilets. When I began hoovering the front room, she got up in that way old people do when they want to remind you how much everything aches and went out, leaving me to it. When she returned an hour later with a stash of women's magazines, she just sat back down in her chair and began reading them without even acknowledging the complete home make-over that had occurred in her absence.'

After clock-watching for several hours, the silence was broken by the phone ringing; it was Walter, asking Les if he'd arrived safely and telling him he'd be home at six. The pair then returned to silence, until Les's mother sprang into action to prepare poached eggs on toast for an imminent Walter.

Walter was glad to see Les, and after catching up over dinner, they sat down to watch Pamela in an episode of *The Professionals*, which was promptly interrupted by the arrival of John and his new girlfriend. John wanted to go to the pub with Les and Walter but Les had insisted on a quiet night in.

Later that evening, Adelaide was in the kitchen when Walter and Les were discussing *The Professionals* and Les commented that it was a shame they'd missed the whole episode. Out of nowhere, the kitchen door burst open and a fuming Adelaide entered, screaming at Les, convinced he had said something about her. He tried to placate her by attempting to hug her but still raging, she yelled at Les not to come near her and picked up the phone to call the police. Walter tackled it from her and Les said he thought it best he left, but Walter defended him and told him if anyone was going to leave, it would be Adelaide. With that, she stormed up to bed and Walter opened a couple of beers.

When Les retired to bed, he noticed the door to the master bedroom firmly closed and was surprised when he heard Walter whisper goodnight from a smaller box room on the other side of the landing; 'I realised then that they were now in separate rooms and I'd come out of a prison and straight back into a warzone!'

The weekend went quick enough. On Saturday, Les's sister Angela came to visit and Adelaide acted as if everything were normal, no further mention was made of her outburst the night before; 'One of her friends came around for a cup of tea and she waxed lyrical like the prodigal son had returned.'

On Sunday, Les, Walter and John went to the pub, where Les was surprised at how much drink John consumed. He initially put it down to having not been in that situation for a while and so perhaps he wasn't really aware how much people drank. When John had previously been to visit Les in Portsmouth, Les had mentioned to Walter how much weight he thought he had gained. When Walter told him he had developed a bit of a drink problem but was getting on top of it, Les blamed himself and his situation, thinking John was struggling with the shame of his brothers incarceration.

The more time Les spent in the house, the more he didn't want to be there, growing more and more anxious and paranoid, blaming himself for John's alcoholism, for Philip's homosexuality, the apparent breakdown of his parents' marriage.

When Tuesday morning came, Les was packed and ready to leave for Wormwood Scrubs, where he was due to report to its hostel, his new home for the next year. The main hostel was located in a large house directly in front of the prison and run by a prison officer. Les was assigned to working in the kitchen serving breakfast and dinner, though for the first few weeks he wasn't permitted to leave at weekends; 'It was essentially a scheme to help you get used to being back in society, giving you the experience of having a job and all its responsibilities, making sure you had somewhere safe to return to and all that. After an initial period, they'd let you go home at the weekend to an address they had to approve but you had to be back indoors by Sunday night so you could be back in the kitchen or wherever you worked first thing Monday morning.'

Les was a model inmate and was soon granted permission to leave at the weekends, but only for one day and he would have to return to the hostel each night. His sister Angela was married to a police officer and so their address was deemed a suitable and safe environment for him to be able to visit. Les was also reunited with Jon Haerem, who was still at the main prison and glad about his progress, gave Les his address so they could remain in touch. Pamela wasn't far either and would invite Les over for Sunday dinner at her home in Earls Court.

One weekend, Les happed to be the only person left in the hostel and not wanting to have to watch him, the prison officer in charge told him he could stay out overnight, provided he was back in time to serve dinner Sunday evening; 'I went to my aunts for dinner and even though I'd written to her and some of the other family members, like my cousin Carol who was there too, it had been years since I'd seen them but it was like no time had passed at all. She was sick with cancer and it showed but she didn't let it stop her cooking a meal for everyone, just like old times.'

After dinner, Les and Carol went for a couple of drinks at a nearby pub where Les was spotted by Dickie Moody, one of the more notorious former inmates from Wormwood Scrubs. Les told him he was now in the hostel, so Dickie congratulated him and slipped him what he assumed was his phone number, telling him if he ever needed anything, to get in touch. Once Dickie had left, Les checked the piece of paper he'd slipped into his pocket to find it was a fifty-pound note.

Back at his aunts, Carol and Les stayed up until the small hours catching up. He told her about the cold reception and erratic behaviour from his mother when he'd first returned home, and she had told her parents who, with no love lost between Joan and Adelaide, wanted to phone her to tell her exactly what they thought of her treatment of Les, but Carol managed to calm everyone down. They suggested perhaps Les should stay with them when he was to be finally granted full weekend leave but Les felt that would make matters worse, so Angela suggested staying with her would be a good middle ground.

Back at the hostel, hearing how much some inmates were earning labouring on the outside, Les had begun looking for work. He had an interview with Callingham's, a painting and decorating company, where he was given assurance that no one would find out from them that he was an ex-prisoner, and it would be in his best interest if he also didn't tell anyone. The following Monday, his first day arrived and he was tasked with cleaning out a garage, burning out paint kettles and cleaning brushes. Les recalled how much that job meant to him and the trust and opportunity that was given to him along with it. His second job with them was in Regents Park, where during a lunch break, one of the other workers told Les that the man who'd hired him had had a son who'd been murdered a few years prior. It gave Les even more gratitude for having been handed the job by a man who knew his history and had experienced such pain and suffering in those circumstances; 'I don't know many men that would have done that. I remember thinking bloody hell, what a man.'

Once Les settled into the routine of his new job, he began to apply to drama schools, but inevitably, most wouldn't give him the time of day in light of his return address. One day, he received a call from a friend who told him one of his idols, Jimmy Cagney, was shooting on the sound stage next to him at Shepperton Studios; 'Armed with a week's worth of sandwiches, my friend snuck me in as a visitor and I sat outside one of those huge buildings all day. Just when I was about to give it up and go home, this big black car pulled up and two important looking fellas got out and marched into the studio. Two minutes later, out they came wheeling an old fart in a wheelchair and as they got closer, I realised it was him, Jimmy!'

Les approached a frail and elderly Jimmy but the two men waved him away, telling him that Cagney was tired. As Cagney climbed into his car, Les shouted out that he was a drama student. Cagney stopped, turned slowly, looked at Les and told him 'It's really quite simple, boy. Know your mark, know your lines and just tell the truth. Good luck, kid.'

Les attempted to rectify the address situation by changing it to his sister's house on correspondence, but after a few weeks, she wrote to him at the hostel to tell him to stop, and that it might be better if he stayed back at home with Walter and Adelaide at weekends. It later transpired that this was due to pressure from Adelaide, keen to control everyone, even if she didn't actually want Les around. The first weekend he was due to stay back home, he went to stay with Louise, where he met a Canadian actress and subsequently ended up back at her hotel; 'This girl travelled the world with a much older boyfriend and she was living in the Royal Lancaster Hotel when I met her. I ended up stopping round there every night after work before getting myself back to the hostel in time for lights out.

Things continued to look up for Les when he received a letter from the Webber Douglas drama school, inviting him to audition for them in a few days' time. Pamela, Mike, Louise and Jeremy all rallied round to help him prepare, and through all the intensity of rehearsals, Les lost his voice twenty-four hours before he was due to perform; 'You've got to gargle port and black pepper, works every time. You can thank Jeremy Young for that one.'

The next morning, Jeremy drove Les to Webber Douglas where upon arrival, he was led into a large hall where he filled out some basic paperwork and waited to be called in. Only one other person was to be auditioned before him. As Les looked around the waiting room, he couldn't help noticing how much older he was than the other people. 'Leslie Grantham', a voice called.

He walked into a room where a panel sat behind a desk, ready to judge him. He opened with a Pinter speech and closed with the Porter's speech; the latter nearly thrown by a coughing fit he fortunately managed to pass off as being part of his performance. A couple of standard questions followed before he was told they would be in touch, and then it was back to Pamela's for a celebration.

Monday came and it was back to the day job. He'd called time on his relationship with the Canadian, who'd returned there to concentrate on being a writer and so it was straight back to the hostel after work. He was returning home to the hostel one evening when he was handed another envelope with 'Webber Douglas Academy of Dramatic Art' printed across it. After a short period of staring at it, he opened it and had to re-read it several times in order for the news to sink in. He immediately phoned his friends to tell them; subject to his release, they were delighted to offer him a place. After he'd spoken with Jeremy, Mike, Pamela and Louise, he called Walter, only for Adelaide to pick up. He told his mum the news but all she could muster was 'I'll tell your dad'.

It hurt but it wasn't enough to dampen the mood, Les was ecstatic, and his friends immensely proud of him.

Apart from valued time with Walter, Les tried to spend as little time as possible at home, instead immersing himself into the creative world of his friends. He continued to work by day painting and decorating, and his old friend Tom, now out and running his own firm, reached out to offer him a full-time job when he was finished in the hostel. Les was allocated a probation officer who asked him what his plans were upon leaving. He handed him the letter of acceptance from Webber Douglas and told him he was going to attend drama school. The probation officer laughed in his face; 'With all the same enthusiasm, I thanked him for his time, got up and left.'

Another probation officer, Andy Marlin, was assigned to Les. He was far more supportive of his plans but was apprehensive about him having an address, given that he didn't want to return home upon his release. Tom had suggested Les talk to a neighbour of his who he knew was looking for lodgers. The probation officer agreed as it was near to where he worked out of, and it would also be convenient for Les to travel to work with Tom.

Les continued to see his sister but would only go home when Walter felt a token visit to appease Adelaide's mood and keep the peace was required. She would claim to be permanently worried that the police would find out he wasn't at home, even though the probation officer was completely aware of his actual location and that he wasn't claiming to be living at home; 'It was a sorry state of affairs and I hated seeing the pressure her behaviour put on dad. If it hadn't have been for him, I'd have stopped having anything to do with that woman long before that.'

Finally, the day Les once thought would never come arrived, and he was released from the hostel. Tom picked him up and drove him to his new home; 'They were a lovely couple that owned the house, Anne and John and they had a kid too, such a generous and kind couple they were.'

As Les settled into bed that night and took a look at the newspaper, the date caught his attention; it was the Thursday 23rd March 1978. His official release date on his licence had been 27th

March but as prisoners weren't released on bank holidays, he had been let out several days early. In that moment, Les remembered Sandhu and the piece of paper he'd given him… '27378'.

The next day, Les contacted Webber Douglas to tell them he was out, and to ask if their offer still stood. He was told he could start immediately, but he had to confess that he didn't yet have the money required to pay his fees. They responded kindly by offering him a scholarship, but he insisted on starting later that summer so he could put a few months' work with Tom under his belt, and be able to pay the fees himself.

By his own admission, working with Tom was hard graft and they worked all hours, sometimes doing one job in the day and another through the night. One evening on his way to a job, Les was walking through Waterloo Station when he was tackled to the ground from behind. As he got up, he was greeted by Buster Edwards, whom he'd been inside with in Portsmouth, and was now running a flower stall on the concourse. Buster asked if he wanted to catch up over a cup of tea, but Les said he was running late getting to his job. 'No worries, old friend', said Buster, 'but you make sure you have a drink on me.'

And just like Dickie had done, Buster slipped Les a fifty-pound note.

While things were on the up for Les professionally and personally, the same could not be said for family life. He was still going to see his parents to appease Walter and keep the peace, but every visit with Adelaide would grate more and more. On one occasion, he stopped by with Louise, around the time she was appearing in *Doctor Who*. Les had asked Adelaide not to tell anyone but he should have known better. When they pulled up outside, half the neighbourhood were out in force wanting photographs and autographs. Les could tell Louise was uncomfortable but she didn't let on to Adelaide, who was insistent she hadn't told anyone.

That year, Les declined many a better offer for Christmas Day and not wanting to leave Walter alone with only Adelaide for company, decided he'd go home. Inevitably, it was a disaster. Walter and Adelaide rowed the whole time and the shouting only intensified when John arrived and subsequently departed within minutes. Boxing Day consisted of awkward silences and an obligatory trip to the local pub where they continued to sit in silence. The next day, Les was on the first train back to London.

CHAPTER EIGHT

Les always said that you can't be taught to act, but a good drama school could certainly contribute to developing talent, and that there were many actors out there that would never perform, simply owing to their own lack of faith in their ability.

When he stepped through the doors of Webber Douglas on his first day, Les was consumed by nerves and anxiety. His first instinct was to try and spot a fellow student from his audition, but he was unsuccessful. What he did note again as he scanned the crowd was that he was again older than the majority of people there, and wondered if perhaps they might look at him and presume he was a teacher, were it not for his matching backpack. During his time there, whenever questioned about why he had joined later in life, he would simply tell people he had been in the army.

Together with the rest of his class, he was led down to the very same room he had auditioned in. There, they were allocated into groups and given a tour of the building and then lunch. There were students there not only from all over the country, but all over the world, and inevitably a lot of attractive young women; 'I felt like a kid in a toy store, all those wonderful things to look at, but no money to be able to buy anything!'

The course was made up of classes in movement, make-up, tap dancing, fencing, speech, voice, singing, text and acting, the latter being based around the Stanislavsky method.

The teachers were a variety of characters, but some stood more firmly in Les's memory than others. He described the principal, Raphael Jago, as a man of vision, always on top of the everchanging nature of acting, and a pioneer for pub and studio theatre. Raphael was assisted by John Malpass, who did far more than his title of Secretary suggested, not only being responsible for the timetable of every student but he was also a counsellor whenever somebody needed to talk.

Roy Riches taught jazz and tap dancing, and loved to wax lyrical about the time he had choreographed a Disney cartoon; 'He was lovely but I wasn't any good at it, so you just sort of tried to stay at the back, out of the way, and not trip anyone up.'

Fencing was taught by Roy Goodall, and his pet dog that would lay at his feet throughout every lesson. The end goal was to acquire a certificate in stage fighting, although on the day of the final exam, with a routine Roy had said was flawless, Les's partner didn't turn up and so he never received his certificate; 'Perhaps the other kid knew it was a waste of time because needless to say, never once in my career have I been asked to provide a certificate before performing a fight!'

Text was taught by Judith Click, a lady for whom Les held great affection. She was in her seventies, but he described her as one of the most beautiful women he ever met, immaculate and exuding class and sophistication. She made him persevere with Shakespeare, something he initially had little interest or understanding of. The end-of-year exam for text involved performing a one person show from the point of view of a character in any Shakespeare story, and Les performed *King Lear* from Kent's perspective, which went on to win him the role of Orsino in the school's performance of *Twelfth Night*.

Robin Winbow taught movement and dance. He was a kind man and a stickler for your shoes matching your costume, so some students would be caught spray painting them in-between classes. Again, it wasn't a class Les excelled at, but Robin could tell, and being a believer that everybody could get better with enough practice, invited Les to his evening classes.

There was a second movement teacher, Caroline, whom Les compared to a young Jane Fonda. Les already had a crush on her and had a hunch it may have been reciprocated; 'Sometimes I'd look up at her during lessons and she'd be looking right back at me. It was wishful thinking that she was dreaming of running off with me and having some love affair, but I thought then it was more likely she was just checking I was keeping up with everyone else!'

It was one evening at the Denmark Arms, the pub of choice for Webber Douglas students, that she had mentioned to Les she was looking for someone to paint her flat. He told her he had worked as a decorator to pay for his tuition, so she invited him round the following evening to give her a quote.

A few weeks after he'd done the job for her, Les decided to throw a party at his place in Wembley and invited all of his classmates. Everybody had a date except Les, so he invited Caroline. She told him she had something else going on in the day but would try and call in on her way back home.

As the evening went on, everyone was having a great time, except for Les, who had realised Caroline obviously wasn't going to be able to make it. The last thing he remembered of that evening was attempting to console himself by taking a puff of someone's joint, his first time, no less. He could vaguely recall hugging the toilet, before he woke up the next morning to find Caroline sitting on the end of his bed. He felt stupid, to say the least. After showering, he went downstairs to find she'd also tidied up. He walked her to the station before returning back to his bed with his tail between his legs, convinced he'd ruined any chance.

As he was preparing for the next day's lessons later that evening, his phone rang. It was Caroline, who told him she was at a bit of a loose end and asked if he'd like to stop by hers for dinner. Trying not to sound overenthusiastic, he dithered about for a moment before accepting. On the way over, he stopped to pick up some flowers, and when he arrived at her place, realised that he should have also bought wine. They then popped to the shops together, and he told me how natural it had felt walking hand in hand with her. Later that evening, she asked him if he knew what a love affair was; she wanted to be with him, but they'd have to keep it a secret. They embarked on their affair and both fell madly in love with each other. He told me that looking back, it had seemed such a shame and so trivial in hindsight, that two people who were so into each other had had to hide something so wonderful.

As the end of the first term arrived, the students put on their first major production, *Tales from the Vienna Woods*; 'Apart from the usual show-offs, we all reckoned we'd been terrible, we were convinced that we'd learned nothing.'

The teachers convened afterwards to assess the performances, while Les went for a swift half in the Denmark Arms before heading back to Caroline's to wait for her. When she finally arrived back, she told him she didn't want to cook and perhaps they should just go grab a takeaway together and have an easy night in. He remembered her holding his hand extra tightly, as if afraid of something, as they walked to the restaurant just around the corner. Les's first thoughts were that he'd been so terrible in the play, she didn't know how to tell him, or worse, that someone had discovered their relationship and she was going to be forced to break it off with him.

When they got back to hers, she told him that at the assessment meeting, one of the other teachers had brought up his past. Now at some point, obviously Jago had consulted with the other teachers about accepting an ex-convict in the first place, but he had never mentioned who. In fact, it had been assumed by many that it was the kid he'd been due to have his stage fight with, because of the way he always arrogantly swaggered about the place. Caroline said no more about it that night, and she kissed him reassuringly and comfortingly when they both left together for school the next morning.

The day started with the students sitting separately with each teacher to hear their thoughts on their performance the previous day. Caroline was the first teacher Les had to sit with; she performed the token gesture of flicking through her notebook, before telling him that she'd give him her more thorough review back at hers that evening. Then came what Les was dreading; having to sit face to face with all of the other teachers now they knew of his past. But none of them mentioned it, save for his acting teacher, Hilary Wood, who told him she loved him even more for knowing what he had overcome.

Jago was the final person to assess Les. His only note was that he'd had a great year and should continue to build upon it. It was clear to Les then, that his past would remain in the past, at least as far as the staff of Webber Douglas were concerned.

Christmas came, and Les worked through most of it decorating with Tom whilst Caroline travelled up north to visit her family. Les went home for a token visit but Walter was the only one who was genuinely pleased to see him. He caught up with friends, including Jeremy, who'd told him he was going to be joining Webber Douglas as a teacher.

On the first day back, it was snowing heavily and Les was forced to walk, the trains even more of a mess than usual. As he entered the classroom for his first lesson of the day, he looked at the clock and saw he was three minutes late. Before he could even open his mouth to apologise, none other than Jeremy Young yelled at him from the stage, demanding to know why he was late.

The next day, he was half an hour early and as he was approaching the main door, saw Jeremy getting out of his car. The two of them ducked into a nearby coffee shop, where Jeremy apologised for having shouted at him. He hadn't known whether any of the other students were aware they were friends already outside of the school and wanted to keep it that way, as he didn't want to be seen as having favourites.

In the new year, there was an obvious shift in the relationship between Les and Caroline. When she returned from having visited her family, Les said she struggled with the balance of teaching all day and then going out with him in the evening, and so they decided to break it off. They would try to recover the relationship several times at Webber Douglas, but always unsuccessfully. Years later, she'd come and see him in plays; sometimes she'd wait at Stage Door, sometimes she would just leave a note.

With an increasing workload at school and a harsh winter consuming London, Les decided it was time to move closer to the school, finding a place in Fulham. He was sad to leave Wembley, and the comfort and convenience of having Tom and his family just over the road, but his new landlord made for the perfect pairing; an older man, he was obsessed with theatre and so took a keen interest in Les and his studies. Les said he had the most fantastic music collection, vinyl records of all of the Broadway showtunes that would be sent to him by a friend in New York, and that he'd always have a homecooked meal ready for him when he arrived home.

With the reduced commute, Les was able to begin saving money, also taking on a couple of odd jobs at the school, cleaning in the mornings and helping processing auditionees on weekends.

Les was still in touch with Jay. She'd moved up north and invited him up to stay with her on his next school break; 'She hadn't aged a day, it was like seeing her for the first time, the first day I realised I was in love with her, all over again.'

That week, they travelled all over the Lake District together, but he realised during that time that no matter how much he thought of her, and though she cared for him deeply, her feelings towards him weren't romantic.

Back at school, the plays were becoming more and more focused on performance. On his fifth term assessment, Jago told him that he was welcome to leave if he wanted. Les being Les, took this as rejection, but what Jago was in fact trying to tell him, was that he felt he was ready to go out into the world on a professional level, and working on a real production would be of more use to him than any further time in a classroom. But Les was determined to receive his degree, so asked to stay, to which Jago agreed, but said he would advance him to finals.

It was as he entered his final term at Webber Douglas that an Australian girl had caught his attention; he described her as a young Vivien Leigh and said she always appeared to be the centre of attention with whoever she was hanging around with. John Lee, a friend of his, had been renting a room from her in a house she owned at the time and told Les that her name was Jane; 'Even just knowing that was enough, there was just something about her. If all I'd ever known about her was just her name, I'd have been quite content.'

One of Jane's friends had asked her if she'd seen 'that guy on lights' when Les was working backstage on a play she was in, and so she'd gone over to try and find out what she could about him. Having seen her mates whispering and giggling behind her, he assumed he was being wound up, so took the opportunity to try his luck and ask her out, thinking he had nothing to lose. She said yes, but he never went, assuming she wasn't going to show up and it was all part of some practical joke.

The next day, she was furious. John Lee had warned Les that she was on the warpath, and so he went to find her and convince her that he had genuinely thought she wasn't going to show. His powers of persuasion worked, and they set another date for the next Friday.

When Friday arrived, the school secretary had come to find Les to tell him she'd received a call for him, and that Walter had been rushed into hospital. As quick as he could, he found John and scribbled a note to Jane, apologising. Needless to say, John decided to 'forget' to give Jane the note and went on the date with her instead.

Walter was suffering from jaundice, but was certainly not on his last legs, as Adelaide had made out on the phone. The doctors reassured Les he wasn't in danger and was going to be fine, and so with the peace of mind from the hospital, and the assumption that John had passed on his note, he headed back home.

The morning after, Jane was again fuming, having been ridiculed by her mates for having been stood up twice by the same man, but once she realised Les was telling the truth about Walter, she calmed down and they scheduled another date.

Their first date was a Saturday night, attending a mutual friends party. On the tube journey there, Les had a brief moment of panic when he realised sat opposite him was a corporal from his regiment in Germany. He recognised Les, but couldn't work out where he knew him from, so Les said hello. They spoke for a while, making small talk until it was clear from the look on this man's face that he had just realised exactly who Les was. There was a brief awkward silence, before he made his excuses and got off; 'Whether it was actually his stop or not, we'll never know, but I doubt it.'

Les and Jane hit it off and were soon an item. He was never able to explain to her why her movement teacher, Caroline, had suddenly taken a dislike to her, but that aside, it was a very happy courtship. It didn't take long for Les to realise this was the woman he wanted to spend the rest of his life with. At the time, she was living in a house just off of the Kings Road and so Les soon moved out of his flat and in with her.

Webber Douglas continued to be more focused and intense. Jane was already working professionally outside of school and well on her way toward getting her Equity card. The students were dividing into cliques more and more, resentment and jealousy setting in. If anyone was lucky enough to be called to an audition or an agent expressed interest, it certainly didn't make them any more liked by their classmates. Castings for plays were like a list of who was the most popular. Les had thought that the school could have been a bit fairer with the process, but hindsight showed him that many of the students that were often given the best roles didn't go on to make it.

Two new teachers, Julia Smith and Tony Holland, joined Webber Douglass in Les's final year to teach television production. The process involved going through scripts for what would later become the television series *Angels*, and learning camera angles, movements and positions. They'd have technical run throughs to understand how a television show was shot from a logistical and technical point of view. As Les was the oldest and Julia could already tell he could clearly act, she made him the show runner. They rehearsed, built a set, and after several successful run-throughs, prepared to shoot an episode.

But on the day of shooting, who should fail to turn up, but the leading man, also known as Les's elusive fencing partner. He'd found out there were some auditions being held for a play on the other side of town and had obviously thought that was a more productive use of his time than television class. So in addition to being responsible for lighting and generally being in charge of the whole affair, Les had to step up and perform the lead role; 'As always, I was convinced I was shit, especially after, when Julia gave everyone notes, she went round the room talking to everyone but said nothing to me. Later on, I found out that she'd agreed with all the other teachers, that television was definitely my forte.'

Julia went on to hire a lot of former students for roles in *Angels,* which would run from 1975 to 1983. She had offered Les a part several times, but he hadn't yet earned his Equity card; 'Little did I know then how much the next time I saw Julia would shape the rest of my life.'

The final term at Webber Douglas consisted mainly of having your headshots taken and reaching out to agents. Les was also appearing in a play in the evenings, *Exhibitions at a Spa,* and would then clean the school afterwards in order to keep some extra money coming in. Without an Equity card, he struggled to get an agent, even with several expressing an interest in him. Jane had recently read a casting breakdown for a part in an upcoming war drama for BBC2 and showed it to Les. She put in a couple of calls and eventually managed to get Les a meeting with the director, Jim O'Brien, and producer, Michael Wearing. Even then, both were heavyweights in television drama and as the meeting went on, the more Les knew he wanted the job. They liked him too and offered him a part on the condition he could acquire his Equity card before shooting. Unfortunately, even with Wearing attempting to pull some strings, he couldn't get it in time, and so Jim O'Brien said they regrettably had to recast the role.

He continued to get call backs and auditions, but every time he would come up against the same issue; 'It's a double-edged sword, because you can't get an Equity card without a body of work under your belt, but you can't get that body of work under your belt without an Equity card.'

By then, John Lee was working at a theatre company and managed to get Les an audition. They offered him a place, but later had to retract the offer once they'd done a background check. He then auditioned for Alan Ayckbourn's company but lost the job when he told a man in the waiting room that he thought Ayckbourne's work was too one-dimensional. It wasn't until he went into the audition room, he realised the man had been Alan Ayckbourn.

Les successfully auditioned for the Belgrade Theatre Company, leading to an offer of three plays, pending his Equity card. Fortunately, Jane came to the rescue, when a friend of her sister offered him three contracts at a club she owned. It was at that time that Jim O'Brien contacted him to see if his circumstances had changed. Although he could no longer offer Les the role they'd originally wanted him for, he and Michael were keen for him to join them on *Jake's End* in a smaller role. He leapt at the opportunity but had to speak to Jago, as the shoot dates would have clashed with what would have been his final showcase performance. Fortunately, he agreed and Les left drama school one day early to pursue his first professional television job.

CHAPTER NINE

True to character, Les had learned not only his lines, but every line in the script, as he headed to Southampton to film his role in *Jake's End* alongside Alan Ford, Derek Martin, P. H. Moriarty and of course John Bindon. The evening of his arrival, he met with Jim O'Brien and the cast and crew in the hotel bar, before retiring early to bed ahead of his 10 a.m. call time. He was eventually called to set in the early evening, after problems caused by Bindon, who had flashed a barmaid in the hotel the night before, and then given an encore to a shopworker in between takes while filming that day.

Les only had one scene, and Jim O'Brien was happy with his performance, receiving an applause when he wrapped; 'That still seemed overboard if you ask me, and I remember watching it when the final one went out and thinking I was terrible, but Jim said I'd done exactly what he wanted, so what can you do?'

A few commercials came along, one for cider and a couple for an insurance firm, which finally brought in a flow of money. Les was also invited back to Webber Douglas to help out with stage management on some pre-final shows, before he travelled up to Coventry to begin his stint with the Belgrade Theatre Company.

The actors came from a variety of backgrounds. For some, like Les, it was their first gig, and others had prominent and successful stage careers, including several members of the Royal Shakespeare Company. The first play was *Whose Life Is It Anyway?* and as Les only had one scene, most of his time during rehearsals was free to explore Coventry.

The play was a huge success and even bigger names joined the company for their second production, *A Little Night Music*, including Kenneth Nelson, Virginia Stride and Pip Hinton, the latter becoming good friends with Les.

As *A Little Night Music* was a musical, extra rehearsal time was needed, so a touring production came into the theatre for a couple of weeks. The star of it was Dave King, and Les had long been a fan of him. He was in the theatre café one day with Raymond Bowers when Dave King had come to eat. Les had asked Raymond if he thought it would be unprofessional to ask for King's autograph, but he said he'd probably be flattered. As Les stood up to approach him, he watched as King yelled and berated a waitress for getting his order wrong; 'That was one of those moments and I saw him and the way he yelled at that poor girl and I swore to myself I'd always try to make time for fans, and I'd certainly never behave like he had to one, to anyone.'

Les didn't return to London often at the weekends, but when he did, he would usually travel by train with the rest of the company, but on one occasion Iain Lauchlan had offered to give him a ride in a van he'd hired to do some moving. On the journey, Iain had mentioned that before setting off, he'd had dinner with his agent. Les asked him if he'd enjoyed the play, to which Iain told him yes, but the main subject of his conversation had been Les; he'd wanted to know if he had an agent yet, and so Les told him about the offers he'd received while finishing up at Webber Douglas, but that none of them had really worked out for whatever reason. Iain told him to get in touch with his agent, as he thought he was genuinely interested.

The very next week, Les had been nursing a coffee in the theatre café when Jill Benedict had come in for lunch with her agent. She asked Les if they wanted to join them; her agent, Bryn, had previously met Les at Webber Douglas, and having seen him in *A Little Night Music*, wanted to take him on.

Although having been contracted for only three productions, the end of their run was followed by the beginning of pantomime season. Les declined a role in the show, but did take the offer of a larger role, three to be specific, at the smaller studio theatre, which was putting on an adaptation of *Lady Chatterley's Lover*.

Before rehearsals began for, Les returned home to Jane, and by this time they'd been living together for a while. Both were in love with each other and so decided to marry one day at the registry office in Fulham. Les phoned Walter immediately after, who was thrilled for him as always, but insisted they also have a proper church ceremony to appease Adelaide. The ceremony was held at the Bolton's Church and Tom served as his best man. Les's former parole officer, Andy, attended, as did Jago, and his old Fulham landlord.

Les said he couldn't recall the ceremony itself as he was so fraught with nerves, but he did remember the moment before Jane arrived and taking in his surroundings; 'I remember turning to my side and seeing Tom, and Jane's brother, and then looking around the church and seeing all these beautiful flower arrangements. I had a flashback to where I'd been only five years before, and then there I was, in this wonderful church, about to marry the love of my life.'

After the ceremony, everybody decamped to a little Italian restaurant in Knightsbridge, before Les and Jane were whisked off for a night at the Ritz Hotel.

Les returned to Coventry to begin rehearsing *Lady Chatterley's Lover* alongside Conrad Asquith and Maureen Beattie. It was such a success that at one point ticket sales were so good there was talk of taking it on tour, but Les said he thought he was so bad in the three roles he was playing, he wouldn't have been asked to return in any of them.

It was in Coventry that Jim O'Brien tracked Les down to tell him he was putting together a series based upon *The Raj Quartet*. The first instalment, *Jewel in the Crown*, was to be filmed in India, and Jim had created a part in it just for him. The casting director said she would speak with his agent and get everything in order.

Lady Chatterley's Lover came to a successful end, and Les returned to London. While waiting for news on *Jewel in the Crown*, he continued to attend auditions and do occasional jobs at Webber Douglas. It was while there, that Les received a phone call from his agent wanting to know why he wasn't at the airport. There had been a breakdown in communication between the production unit in India and Granada in Manchester, but as at the time Granada was constantly flying people back and forth for the production, Les was put on a flight two days later, but still two weeks earlier than he'd originally been told.

Les recalled touching down in Delhi in the early morning, and that first feeling of the heat hitting you when you step off the plane, even though it was still dark. His first day there was spent being given a guided tour of the sights, and after returning to the hotel for lunch, Les asked his driver to show him the other side of the city; the slums and the poverty, which he told me were one of the worst things he'd seen.

The following morning, he met in the hotel lobby with actor Albert Moses while they waited for their transport to take them to Shimla, some eight hours north, where they'd stay at the Woodville Palace Hotel, where filming was to take place. That evening, Granada threw a party for the cast and crew and Jim O'Brien introduced Les to his castmates. Before having left London, a friend of Les's had asked him to give his regards to Geraldine James, who was playing the female lead. Eventually spotting her in the crowd that night, he began talking to her and was passing on his friends message when he was approached by the male leads, Charles Dance and Tim Piggot-Smith, both of whom were displeased at Les, whom they perceived to be a minor player, talking to their leading lady. Given his only scene was to be with Charles Dance, he thought it best to not aggravate the situation any further, made his excuses and retired to bed early.

When Les arrived on set the next morning, Dance was still cold with him. Their scene involved him leading Les around a building and crossing a parade ground until they reach another building, where Dance's character then meets Geraldine. Most of the dialogue was Les's and they rehearsed the scene several times until Jim was happy, and then went for a take. Before calling action, Charles leant into Les and suggested that perhaps the scene might look better if Les took the lead and walked slightly ahead of him. Jim shouted 'Action!' and Les took the lead prompting Jim to yell 'Cut!' before he could even get his lines out. They reset.

As the camera's began rolling again, Dance whispered another suggestion and told Les it might look better if he started his dialogue once they were in the full sunshine. 'Action!'... 'Cut!'.

Les thought he was about to get sacked from the way Jim O'Brien threw down his script and marched up to him, but then he turned on his heel to Charles Dance, telling him to let Les do the scene the way he had rehearsed it; 'He told him it wasn't his scene, it was mine, and he hadn't flown me all the way across the world to play second fiddle to him. He never spoke to me again, but for what it's worth, I thought he was very good in it...'

Once the rushes report was received the next day, Les was wrapped and made his way back to England. On the plane home, he couldn't help feeling lucky and taking stock. At this point, he'd been out of drama school for just over a year and now had two television dramas under his belt, four well received plays and a handful of advertisements. And of course, he now had his Equity card.

Upon returning to London, Les took up a bar job while continuing to audition. He also walked the streets looking for an additional day job, but though the offers were plentiful, employers were less interested when Les told them he was an actor and would need to take time off from time to time for auditions. Eventually, he found work in a small greengrocers in South Kensington; 'It wasn't the best paid job in the world, but Peter that owned the shop was supportive enough when I'd have an audition or call back, plus at the end of the week, I'd be able to take home to Jane whatever food was left over that we hadn't been able to sell, and it was better than signing on.'

After a few months at the greengrocers, he was headhunted by a customer who owned an Italian tailor, Piero de Monzi, where Les would serve the likes of Eric Clapton, Lady Diana, Bob Geldoff and Dustin Hoffman.

Michael Wearing reached out to Les to tell him he was developing a television drama, to be directed by the actor Richard Wilson. He had two parts in mind for Les, but after auditioning for an unimpressed Wilson, Les got neither.

He then auditioned for the part of a prisoner in a play at the Bridge Lane Theatre but was turned down because the director didn't think he looked like he could be convincing as a prisoner.

Just as he was starting to question his career, he was offered a part in a play directed by Dutch director Laurens Postma, which led in turn to filming two sitcom pilots for Central & ATV at Elstree.

Les then appeared in an episode of *Good Night and God Bless* alongside Donald Churchill and Jude Lowe, something he recalled being doomed from the beginning but notable for, if anything, the debut of Leslie Ash.

In 1985, Debbie McWilliams cast Les in *Morons from Outer Space*, starring Mel Smith and Griff Rhys Jones. Les thought it was absolutely awful but remembered the only line he had getting a lot of laughs at the premiere.

Matthew Robinson invited Les and Jane to lunch to ask if he would be interested in appearing as the lead villain in an episode of *Doctor Who* he was going to be directing. He accepted immediately, but while terms were being worked out between the BBC and his agent, John Nathan Turner, the then executive producer of the show had dismissed the idea of Les, because he didn't feel he was a big enough star. Matthew had tried to fight Les's corner but to no avail, but Turner did agree to Les being given a smaller role in the episode, that of Kiston.

At the time, Peter Davidson was the The Doctor and Rula Lenska also appeared in the episodes with Les. Filming took several days and Les enjoyed it immensely, especially his time with Rula, whom he said was great fun.

While at the BBC, he got word of a show called *Knock Back* being in development, and with the help of the *Doctor Who* floor manager Corinne Hollingworth, managed to get an audition. The two leads had already been cast in the drama about a prisoner and his relationship with a social worker, the former to be played by Derek O'Conner and the latter by Pauline Collins. After delivering his best Tempest's speech from *Forty Years On* to Piers Haggard, he eventually gave Derek another part in the series and Les won the lead role alongside Collins.

CHAPTER TEN

After *Doctor Who*, Matthew went on to direct *Coronation Street* and offered a part to Les that would have seen him have an affair with Bet Lynch, but he turned it down, not wanting to do a soap. Not to be discouraged, Matthew contacted Les again a few months later with a not too dissimilar proposition; Julia Smith and Tony Holland were putting together a new soap for the BBC set in London, then titled *East 8*, and had asked for his help in casting. He wanted to put Les forward and not wanting to appear ungrateful, Les said yes. He met with Julia and Tony, neither of whom mentioned remembering him from Webber Douglas, and read for the part of a barrow boy, Pete.

Les was barely through his door when he received a call from Matthew, congratulating him on getting the part of Den. He told Matthew he had auditioned for the part of Pete, but Matthew was adamant he was to play Den. A few days later, he received a letter from Julia, which read '*I thought you might like to be put out of your misery, so I am writing this brief note to say that all being well and other things being equal, I hope you will be joining us on 'East 8' to play the part of Den.'* At the bottom of the letter, handwritten were the words '*Long live the W.D.!*'

Over the next few weeks, Les would join Julia and Tony at the production offices in Shepherds Bush, to read alongside other actors still being considered for various roles. Les was told not to let any of the other actors he read with know that he had the part, in case it affected their performance. Two of the people he read alongside were Letitia Dean and Jean Fennell, the latter he recalled being somewhat intense and quite hard work. He remembered walking the pair of them to the tube station after their audition and him and Letitia barely able to get a word in as Jean told them how she was going to be the star of the show and the new Bet Lynch; 'They were getting tubes in different directions and Jean's came first. She got on and we waved her off, then Tish and I just looked at each other and shook our heads.'

A month later, Les attended the first official cast meeting at BBC Elstree. The first order of business was deciding what kind of a dog Den would have. Julia and Tony came up with the obvious suggestions; rottweilers, alsatians, etc. Les jokingly suggested a poodle might be more in keeping, which got a laugh and Julia told him to have a think about it over the weekend and see if he had any more sensible suggestions.

Rehearsals weren't due to start for several weeks, and because Les's contract with *EastEnders* was only for a handful of episodes, his agent continued to send through offers for other projects.

The first day of rehearsals arrived and the cast all met at Television Centre, and together with some of the crew, took one of the BBC's shuttle buses to Elstree. Scripts were handed out and they began a read-through. The plan was to work on the first episode's script for several weeks before filming would actually commence. The cast were invited to the wardrobe department to look over clothing and jewellery that they thought might be appropriate for their characters. Les picked a watch and Julia agreed with his choice. Jean was still, in her mind, determined to be the next Bet Lynch, as was reflected in her costume choices, until Julia told her in no uncertain terms, not to question her about a character she had invented.

The cast were given a tour of the lot and Albert Square itself, designed by the wonderful Keith Harris. Letitia, Jean and Les were shown the Vic for the first time and Les was alarmed to see upon closer inspection that the walls were adorned with Arsenal memorabilia. Les took umbrage and so the next day the photographs were replaced with pictures of West Ham players.

Everyone rehearsed for several weeks, nailing some key scenes, then rehearsing with cameras and recording little bits here and there before filming of the first episode would take place.

Les recalled gathering with the other cast in the greenroom at 10 a.m. before heading onto set to deliver his immortal opening line… 'Stinks in 'ere'.

Once taping was finished, Julia, Tony and Matthew all went off into a meeting, before Julia returned and told everyone to go home. Les had the distinct feeling she wasn't satisfied with something, and it being his nature to worry about such things, assumed it was him and returned home to await the inevitable phone call telling him he was sacked.

That evening, the phone indeed rang. Jane answered, then passed it to Les. It was Matthew, who said he was calling with bad news; Julia and Tony weren't happy with Jean and were looking for a replacement immediately; 'Thing is, apart from that day at the tube station and the incident with wardrobe, when she was acting and in front of the camera, I thought she was fine, wasn't doing anything wrong, and really was alright to get along with, but whatever it was she was doing, Julia didn't like it, and what she said, went.'

Some of the other female cast members who hadn't yet taped their own scenes asked Julia if they could be considered for the role, but each one was told they were either too old or too young or just not right to play opposite Les, at which point a couple of them provided Julia with suggestions of actors who could replace Les. This wasn't well received by Julia.

The very next day in the canteen, Les was eating breakfast when Julia introduced him to Anita Dobson. The three went onto the lot where they were joined by Tony, and they ran through a scene that Les and Jean had struggled with previously. Something clicked and it just felt right, so they repeated it in costume and on camera and there was a round of applause from the crew. That afternoon, there was a technical run for a full episode, and then Julia and Tony would go into a meeting with the writers to make notes.

The next morning, Matthew delivered those notes to the actors, and so they'd rehearse and re-block certain scenes that hadn't worked the day before, and then they were reshot.

Mondays and Tuesdays were used for readthroughs, rehearsals and blocking, Wednesdays and Thursdays were studio interior filming days and Fridays would be exterior filming days on the lot. Saturday's were also rehearsals. A typical filming day in the early days of the show would begin with an 8 a.m. call time, and from then till noon would be camera rehearsals. After lunch, they'd film until 4 p.m. before breaking for dinner and then filming until 10 p.m.

Press and publicity were beginning to build around the show and having seen some early episodes, Michael Grade had asked Julia and Tony to push Den and Angie to the forefront of it all. This led to Les asking Jane if he thought it was a good idea to mention his past to Julia and Tony. He ran it by Matthew, who listened to what he had to say without any judgement whatsoever and agreed that it was appropriate to tell Julia sooner rather than later.

A couple of weeks into filming, Les's agent called him to tell him his contract had been extended to a full year. Several actors were let go, not because they weren't good, but because when it came to consider the longevity of some of the storylines, they just didn't have legs. Julia and Tony had seen enough at this point to know what was working and what wasn't.

The official launch day finally arrived, and the cast assembled at Television Centre to be interviewed. Peter Dean introduced everyone before they took questions, though Les recalls most of them being directed at Wendy Richard and Shirley Cheriton.

Everybody was then shuttled back to Elstree, where they gathered for a viewing of the first episode. Les struggling to watch himself and instead focused on the reactions of a man sat next to him, who he said he didn't recognise, nor had he seen him before. After the screening finished, the man had turned to Les and shook his hand, congratulating him and asking what he thought. Les told him it was alright, but the music was terrible. The man then introduced himself as Simon May, the composer.

The next day, February 19th 1985 at 7 p.m., the first episode of *EastEnders* aired. While the rest of the cast and crew gathered in the BBC Club to watch the event, Julia Smith stayed home. Roly, who portrayed Den's poodle, lived with Julia, and just before seven, he decided he needed to go out. As she walked him down her street, she heard the theme tune coming from every house they passed.

That evening, Les, Jane, Matthew and his girlfriend celebrated with a meal, before returning home to learn lines ahead of the 8 a.m. call time the next morning. The phone rang all night with people calling to congratulate Les, but the only one he really cared about was Walter, who he said was completely choked with pride.

When Les arrived for work the next day, he couldn't help noticing a woman dressed to the nines like a Hollywood star, disguised by a dramatic hat and sunglasses. It was Shirley Cheriton, who had seemingly let the reviews, that everyone else was sat around reading while giving themselves a pat on the back, go to her head.

On set, Peter Dean turned up, and while in between takes, made small talk with Les. Les had asked what he had done the night before and Peter told him he'd been in his brother's nightclub and bumped into someone who claimed they were good mates with Les. When he asked who, Peter told him 'a chap by the name of Frank O'Connell. Knows you really well, apparently'.

Not only had Frank been in Wormwood Scrubs with Les, but Frank was also the only person he'd had a fight with inside. Before Les could respond to Peter, the director began shouting instructions and the pair went back to work.

The next day, Adam Woodyatt was the first person Les saw, and Adam asked him if he'd seen Letitia Dean or Susan Tulley. Apparently, Peter had said something to them about Les's past that had upset them. He went to find the pair immediately. They asked him if it was true, and he said it was and understood if they didn't want to talk to him. They were both supportive. The next person Les went looking for was Peter. He let Adam know he was looking for him, and Adam apparently made the mistake of mentioning to Peter why Les was looking for him; within fifteen minutes, Peter Dean was carted off in an ambulance, having suffered a heart attack in reception.

Les felt terrible until Peter waltzed in the next day looking good as new, his heart attack turning out to have been a bad, but convenient case, of indigestion. Les told him never to talk about him or his business as he had to Letitia or Susan again, and wanted to know why he'd only chosen to tell the younger members of the cast. He never forgave Peter for that, even though in the last few years of Les's life, Peter reached out on numerous occasions to try and make amends.

A few days later, Les was in the canteen when he was told he had a phone call. He picked it up assuming it would be an internal call, but it was a journalist from The Sun, wanting to know about his time in prison. He hung up and called Jane immediately, and she told him not to worry. He then went straight to Cheryl, who was in charge of the press department and had also been contacted. By the end of the day, the studio was surrounded by a sea of journalists. Les met with Julia, who was trying to compose a statement. He offered his resignation, but neither her, Tony or Michael Grade would accept it, insisting they would ride out the storm together.

That evening, Matthew smuggled Les out of the studios in the boot of his car and dropped him off on the corner of his street. Journalists were already surrounding the house too and had been shouting through the letterbox at Jane all day, wanting to know what it was like to live with a killer. She was in floods of tears by the time he eventually managed to get past them and through the front door.

The next day, the front pages of every newspaper were full of every variation of 'EastEnders star a killer'. The house and the studios were constantly surrounded. Matthew picked up Les and drove him to the studios, where he pinned a letter he'd composed to the noticeboard in reception. In the letter, he apologised to his fellow cast and said he understood if any of them weren't comfortable working with him anymore.

Julia gathered the cast in the studio and when Les arrived, Wendy Richard was the first to come up and hug him. When he next saw the noticeboard, his letter had been removed and none of the cast mentioned it again.

In the weeks that followed, it was all the papers could talk about, demanding that the BBC sack him and condemning them for standing by a criminal who had taken a life. Everyone from childhood friends to inmates to people who'd never even met him were selling their stories, and it was all printed as gospel.

While Les was protected to some degree by the sanctuary of being in a studio all day, the same couldn't be said for Jane, who became unable to leave the house without being hounded and harassed, and they had to live with the curtains permanently closed.

EastEnders was a ratings winner and a huge success for the BBC. When Michael Grade moved it to its later 7.30 p.m. slot, the viewing figures continued to climb and Les was offered countless public appearances; what were only supposed to be one or two hour engagements turned into all day affairs, as mobs of people would queue around the block to meet him.

The public couldn't get enough of Den and Angie, so after the show had been running a while and had cemented itself in popular culture, Julia pitched Les and Anita something that had never been done before; she wanted an episode devoted to just the two of them. Les wasn't convinced it would work, because he felt soaps only worked on a formulaic level of not being terribly demanding or taxing on the attention of the audience. Then Julia pitched her storyline; Angie was going to announce to Den that she only had six months left to live. Den, racked with guilt for having been cheating on her with Jan, would then take her to Italy, only for Angie to mistake this guilt for genuine love and confess to Den that she had made up the illness. Den would then respond by serving Angie with divorce papers on Christmas Day.

For Les and Anita as actors, it was a dream come true; 'It might be just a soap, but back then, in the beginning, it was huge, you have to remember there were only a couple of channels. We were in everyone's living rooms, it had such an impact.'

Les continued to make an impact and make headlines. He was selective over which papers he sued. If it was something wildly defamatory, he'd take action, but avoided suing over any articles pertaining to his criminal history; 'It's very hard to go near that without having the whole thing dragged up each time and you can't take a story like that and start dissecting which parts are true and which aren't. At the end of the day, I did it, and I'll always have to live with the shame of it, rightly so, but that's always, to me, been between me and my maker, not the readers of The Sun.'

A lot of cast members that had left were selling stories; 'You had these actors that thought it was going to last forever, which, obviously, nothing does. Suddenly they were out of work, but they still had bills to pay and they knew *EastEnders* sold papers. None of the stuff they printed was true, of course not, who would want to read about how lovely everyone was to each other?'

By this time, Les and Jane had two phones; one personal and one business. Les had instructed the BBC Press Office to not call him every time a paper had asked for a comment or response from him, as he had a rule of never responding to any of them. One evening, a journalist had phoned directly, asking if he had any comments regarding the allegations that were going to be printed the next day. He hung up, thinking it would be no more fictional nonsense than usual.

The next day, he pulled into the petrol station on his way to work and saw the headline 'Dirty Den is a Racist'. Sally Sagoe, an actress from the show, had left and as was to be expected, sold the story of her time there to the highest bidder. When interviewed, she had accused Les of calling her 'a man in a frock'. Sally had been brought into *EastEnders* to play the wife of Tony Carpenter as Oscar James been struggling to keep up with the fast turnaround and learning lines. Her dressing room had been next to Les's and one day she'd come in to run some lines with him and to ask his advice. Les looked over her script and could clearly see where Tony's name had been erased and her character's name written in its place, but no changes had been made to the dialogue. Les had jokingly told her that unless she wanted to sound like 'a man in a frock', she should make some tweaks to her lines, so they sounded more suited to her. That was then turned into something it clearly wasn't but went some way toward backing up the papers claim he was a racist. As for the racism, there had been a scene in the Vic where Den was to use the phrase 'big sooty horse', but Les had pointed out to the writer that it had racist connotations and so the scene was reshot with the phrase 'big black horse'. However, the notes didn't get to the editor and so the 'big sooty horse' take was the version broadcast. Combine that, with Sally, as a black woman, confirming that it was a racist remark and this racist had also accused her of looking like a man in a frock and there's your story. As Les was walking back to his car, several black men got out of the vehicle behind him, all carrying newspapers. They were all thrilled to meet him and even asked him to sign their papers; 'I asked one of them who he wanted it made out to, and he told me 'just put Sooty!' and laughed.'

It was around this time that the character of Michelle was to fall pregnant. Les had originally thought the father was going to be her brother Mark, as at the time the two characters were sharing a bedroom and knowing how ground-breaking Julia and Tony were with their storylines, it seemed like the obvious scenario. Julia and Tony met with Les and told him it was to be Den and later, Susan Tulley approached him in the canteen and told him she was glad it was him.

The day before filming the famous reveal scene at the canal, Julia was told at the last minute that she would not be able to use her usual crew and a special film unit would be used, which jeopardised the secrecy of the shoot. She was so angry that she threatened Michael Grade with her resignation, but they ended up compromising that she could use her usual crew for the canal scenes, but a film unit would be needed for the upcoming Venice shoot.

The shoot went without a hitch, with the exception of the rain. The heavens opened while rolling and so Les decided to go with it, and nudged Susan toward the bridge. The cameras were reset to shoot the remainder of the scene there, with Julia proud to point out that a film crew would not have been able to keep up with the pace of their resets on location. The episodes were a huge success and another ratings winner, the storyline affirming the tabloids obsession with 'Dirty Den.'

As the Venice shoot approached, Jane was at home heavily pregnant with their first son, Spike. Les had booked his holiday around the due date but a mix-up with scheduling meant a lot of fraught negotiating between Les and his agent, and Julia and the BBC, when he was told at twenty-four hours' notice that he was to be in Venice the next day. Someone, somewhere, had dropped the ball, but on the promise of Les being flown home immediately upon news of Jane going into labour, things were resolved at the eleventh hour. The BBC had organised for a press conference at Heathrow first thing in the morning when Les and Anita were due to fly out, and it was the inevitable circus.

In Italy, there was no respite from the journalists, following the production everywhere and even taking over entire hotels. Unable to avoid them, Les ended up breaking protocol and sitting down for a drink with them one night, on the condition they didn't ask him any questions. They were unusually good on their word and didn't, and it was by all accounts, a convivial evening. The shoot concluded on the Orient Express and Julia, who directed all of the Venice episodes couldn't have been happier.

The press always gave Julia a hard time, but her and Les were very close and you could always see the pride on his face when he spoke of her and what they all achieved together, back then. But at the end of the day, had it not been for her and Tony, none of it would have come to pass. So, despite the tabloids dislike of her, she was justifiably rewarded with a BAFTA for her outstanding contribution to television.

When Princess Diana came to visit the set, she remembered Les from Piero de Monzi and they exchanged correspondence for a while. She was keen to pursue a friendship with him, but he declined several invitations, not wanting the added press intrusion that it would have brought. It was at that time that the stories were growing more and more personal, and Jane and Les were inevitably getting more and more paranoid, as to whether someone close to them, other than his family, were behind the leaks. It was only one evening, when someone had called the house and after picking up the phone and it continued to ring, that it dawned on them that their phone had been bugged. A B.T. engineer, always the same one, would come but could never seem to fix the problem, so eventually Les hired a private engineer who found the phones had been bugged by the B.T. engineer.

A few weeks after, Les had put his car in for a service and because he had a public appearance the following day, asked the prop master on *EastEnders* if he could borrow a car, to avoid the hassle of going to a rental firm. He drove home in the car he had been lent, and as he parked it outside his house, two men, both armed, wrestled him to the ground. Fortunately, they were undercover police; 'Turned out there'd been a threat on my life, some nut had phoned in to the BBC to say he was going to shoot me, but Julia hadn't told me because she didn't want to worry me and more importantly Jane, so she'd gone to Michael Grade and they'd organised for some plain-clothed police to keep an eye on me. They didn't know I'd put our car in for a service, why would they, so when they saw this white Rover pulling up and assumed it was the gunman coming for me!'

There was as much drama happening off-screen as there was on, and Les was getting tired of it all. The cast had divided into cliques, there was a lot of resentment and a lot of people taking themselves very, very seriously; 'You have to remember how big it was back then, so no matter how small a role someone played in it, just by association with *EastEnders*, they all thought they were bloody amazing, everyone thinking they had that job that if they didn't turn up, the whole thing would have fallen apart, and you have to remind yourself that on a machine like *EastEnders*, no one is bigger than the show.

People were getting complacent, greedy and lazy, and after a couple of days in a row of Les being the first in and spending too much time waiting around for other people to stroll in throughout the day, at their own leisure, with the most ludicrous excuses, Les snapped. No one was taking their job seriously anymore and taking all the perks that came with it for granted. He went up to Julia's office and told her he'd had enough and wanted to leave. A couple of days later, Anita had the same meeting with Julia. Shaw was initially upset at Les announcing he wanted to leave but when Anita said the same thing, for a moment she thought it was a ploy between the pair to get more money. Julia went back to Les and told him that after discussions with the BBC, if she was able to persuade either him or Anita to stay, they wanted it to be Les. He was determined to move on from the show, so phoned Michael Grade, who by this time had moved on to Channel 4, and asked his advice. Michael recommended he helped Julia out by at least staying for a couple of weeks.

Being as in creative as she was, Julia decided that in the six weeks Les was going to stay, she would pull off one more audacious shoot; she would film a year's worth of storylines for Den in that time frame. Bill Lyons, a favourite writer of Les was drafted to write 'Den's Story' which would be shot on location, including Dartmoor Prison, and then the scenes would be inserted into the episodes throughout the year. However, when Julia had gone to Dartmoor to recce ahead of filming, she was told that ex-prisoners weren't permitted back inside as visitors. After negotiating with the prison Governor, a compromise was reached, that filming could take place on the condition the prisoners were able to watch filming.

Every day of filming in Dartmoor Prison was hectic due to the scripts still being finished as late as the night before, meaning Les wouldn't get them until 10 p.m. and some were even being rewritten on location. Julia had created a whole new group of characters that would exist alongside Den in prison, as well as John Altman and Michael O'Hagan. Les also managed to land Jeremy Young a part of a prison officer, as a thank you for all he had done helping him through drama school.

As always, Julia did a fantastic job of rallying the troops and Les held her responsible for pulling off such an ambitious shoot, something in his mind, no one else could have done. On the first day of shooting they managed to get thirteen minutes in the can and by the time the last day came, they were filming just shy of forty minutes each day; 'As you know, she was an incredible, formidable force and taught me everything I know about television. Hers was the only funeral I attended other than my own father's when I really felt like something in me changed, I lost something, I lost a part of me.'

Driving back to London after the last day's filming, Les was looking forward to whisking a pregnant Jane off on holiday to Italy, when his agent called him, asking him if he had time in the morning before his flight, to go to the Royal Lancaster Hotel and meet with a Scottish director about a new drama series called *Winners and Losers.*

After a hurried meeting, the director gave him a couple of scripts to read on holiday and Les headed out to Heathrow. By the time he returned, the contract was already among his mail, Michael having done the deal while he was away.

Before filming in Glasgow commenced, Les was invited to take part in a campaign to save the Rose Theatre. The Rose dated back to Shakespeare, and while builders had been excavating for foundations for a new office block, had stumbled across its remains.

The likes of Olivier and Gielgud had been involved in the campaign, recording sonnets from their favourite works; 'If I'd have taken to the stage and started doing my Hamlet, the bulldozers would have been in like a shot!'

That didn't deter them and Les was invited to perform alongside Vanessa Redgrave, Ian Charleson, John Alderton, Timothy and Janet McTeer. Dustin Hoffman was even in the audience and with queues for autographs from all round the block, the evening was a huge success. It was also that night that Les was introduced to Chris Villiers, someone who would become a lifelong friend. After a six-degrees-of-separation story about Boots and cricket, Chris invited him down to play with his team, The Wandsworth Cowboys, a motley crew of actors, writers and directors. A stone's throw from their home, those cricket matches became something of a sanctuary for Les and Jane, and it gifted him the opportunity to play alongside some incredible names over the years, from Hugh Laurie to Sam Mendes.

There was one more scene to film before Les could head to Glasgow; his death scene for *EastEnders*, famously gunned down by a bunch of daffodils. It was a complicated shoot. Instructions misunderstood, the flowers were forgotten until the very last minute and the man who had been cast to play the gunman had become so wrapped up in being the man who would kill Dirty Den, that he had sold his story to a tabloid and had to be replaced at the last minute. The first assistant director was dating John Nathan Turner and couldn't resist telling Les that 'John always said he knew you'd be a star', which was interesting considering he hadn't given him the time of day on *Doctor Who*, 'That's the wonderful thing about producers, always oh so wise, but only after the event, it amazes me that anything gets made at all.'

A shot of Den landing in the water was filmed in the water tank at Ealing Studios, where Keith Harris had re-created the canal right down to shopping trollies and old bikes, but the shot was never used when it was decided to leave the ending more ambiguous. Perhaps that wasn't to be the last of Den after all?

CHAPTER ELEVEN

When Les arrived in Scotland to film *Winners and Losers*, he was treated like royalty; taxi drivers refused to charge him fares, no restaurant or bar would take his money and he even managed to prevent Celtics and Rangers fans battering each other, when after a match, they had descended upon the city centre and saw Les filming, instead forming queues for autographs and to watch the production.

He had a few sex scenes with actress Denise Stephenson and the following evening when her agent had taken her for dinner, keen for gossip, she'd asked her what Les was like in bed. Naturally, her response was along the lines of 'well I'm not really sure, because he kept his underwear on', but the tabloid headlines the next morning were 'Dirty Den Keeps His Pants On In Bed'. All the work of an agent trying to get her clients name out there, not content with her already being the female lead of the show. The agent in question happened to be Sharon Hamper, who would infamously go on to be banned from running such an agency after pocketing nearly half a million pounds of her client's money, including that of Caroline Quentin, Leslie Ash and Craig McLachlan.

Winners and Losers was a critical success and reviews were still coming in when Les received the scripts for *The Paradise Club*, which would go on to be, after *EastEnders*, one of the projects he spoke about with so much pride and amassed quite the cult following.

Les was travelling to see Walter regularly, but with his relationship with Adelaide strained, they would usually meet in the pub around the corner, and he would travel on his own to Wimbledon to see them at the house. He was heavily involved in local politics at the time and many people were asking him to be mayor but he didn't feel it was the appropriate time, with the strain of his failing marriage and instead, was putting his support behind a friend he felt better suited to the position. The press also gave Walter a hard time and having taken up such a position himself, it would only have brought more unwanted attention from the tabloids. Whilst Walter had always refused to talk to them, the same could not be said for Adelaide, who was often spotted leaving the back door to join reporters in their cars.

Angela's marriage had broken down and John's marriage was also under strain and their respective partners also took to selling stories to the press. Angela had moved in with John under the guise of wanting to help him through his marital woes, but it was obvious to Les it was because she didn't have anywhere else to go.

Press intrusion for Les was also creeping back up to an *EastEnders* level. He was being driven back home after filming *The Paradise Club* when he picked up a newspaper on the back seat to read the headline 'Dirty Den Disowns Niece and Her Black Baby!'

It transpired that Angela's daughter, Claire, whom Les had no contact with, was living happily with a black man she was married to, and they had had a baby. Reading that headline was the first Les had heard of the situation, the relationship, the baby. A few days later, another story appeared claiming that Les and Jane had stopped Adelaide from seeing her grandchildren. This was correct, owing to Adelaide having sided with Angela about her having also been selling stories, but it confirmed to Les that it had been her that had sold the story about him disowning the baby. Hastily, and in anger, he phoned Adelaide as soon as he arrived home, which then in turn prompted her to phone the press once more. That evening, when Walter had come home, he found Adelaide in the living room talking merrily away to a journalist and photographer about how awful Les was. Walter threw the pair out of the house and before he could even begin to yell at Adelaide, she left of her own volition to continue the conversation with them around the corner. After that, Les vowed she would never see him or his children again. Walter and Adelaide's relationship only deteriorated further from that point.

The BBC loved *The Paradise Club* and had already commissioned a second series before the press night for the first, at which there was a standing ovation. However, the next day a newspaper ran a story slamming the inappropriate nature of a scene, given his past, in which Les shot a man in the head. No scene like this existed, so the production company contacted the newspaper editor to challenge the article. The editor and journalist both adamantly stood by the story and Zenith sent them a copy of the episode in full to show the scene didn't exist. The newspaper responded by accusing Zenith of having deleted the scene from the supplied copy and so Zenith threatened legal action, at which point they backed down, but, of course, never retracted the story.

At a lunch with producer Mark Shivas, Les was asked what he thought of *EastEnders*, as at the time, it was suffering from declining viewing figures. Les thought it had become stale where other soaps had successfully tried to step up their game. Shivas asked if he'd consider returning as a producer, but Les didn't feel it would be appropriate, and would have caused friction with the cast, given he felt a cull was needed in order to get things back on track. Shivas was also a fan of *The Paradise Club* but felt a third series would be unlikely, given its spiralling costs. Les proposed that it could be a co-production, produced by Zenith and using BBC staff, but Shivas dismissed the idea, saying such a thing would never happen. A year later, it did, when the BBC produced its first co-production, using external companies with internal staff. Jonathan Powell, the then Head of Drama, then cancelled *The Paradise Club* after its second series was successfully transmitted.

Les suggested that Corinne Hollingsworth, the then production associate on *EastEnders* should be made producer, and she was, but all of these moves where happening with everyone's aligned goal; to get Les to return to *EastEnders*. Unfortunately, it wasn't his goal, and every headline printed about him confirmed his decision to not return.

Les and Jane were about to return to her family in Australia for another holiday, when director Paul Elliot requested a meeting with him. Elliot had wanted him for the lead in *Rick's Bar*, the play on which his favourite film *Casablanca* had been based. Paul had first offered the role to Albert Finney, but he had turned it down, saying it was unplayable. Les said he was interested but needed to read the script in full and would do so on holiday. Les was only in Australia for a couple of days when his agent contacted him, to tell him the deal had already been done, as they were moving their dates forward. The press jumped on the announcement of Les's casting by trying to say the production was plagued by issues, but as usual, none of the stories were true. Les's leading lady, Ilsa, was played by Shelley Thompson, who had been at RADA while Les was at Webber Douglas, but she had also been a former housemate of Jane's.

Opening night was completely sold out and was even attended by Murray Burnett, the original author of the play, who had nothing but kind words. Jane's family had also flown in from Australia for the occasion, her father also being a huge fan of the original film. The production then moved to the Whitehall Theatre, where reviews continued to praise the production and Les's performance. Lance Percival read a review by Jack Tinkler and had sent a bottle of champagne to Les along with a note which read, *'With a review like that, you can now retire'.* Paul had forwarded Tinkler's review to Albert Finney, with a note which simply read, *'No, it isn't...'*

A few years later, Jack would tell Les in person that his performance as Rick had been one of the most accomplished he'd ever seen.

At one performance, the curtain went up and Les was met by the sight of row upon row of audience members dressed in white dinner jackets, who at the intermission, got up and began chanting 'Better than Bogie!', which Les said although flattering, was probably very much an exaggeration.

The money wasn't great, but it was still money and Les knew he was involved in something good. That was, until Paul Elliott took him to one side and told him that everybody would need to take a pay cut in order to keep running in the West End, and that the current cast costs were astronomical. This set off a red flag for Les, thinking it strange given every night continued to be a sell-out performance. But something had to give and within a few weeks, the play closed.

Despite Les's affection for the project and the kudos it brought him, he was quick to dust himself off and get on with things. He did a film for Channel 4, and then had his pick of pantomime that winter, settling on *Babes in the Wood* in Nottingham.

Rehearsals, Les recalled, were somewhat like a sitcom. A few days in, the director phoned Les to ask if he could sing. He said he couldn't, so was surprised when a few days later he received the lyrics for the song he was to sing. The next day, the director called him to ask if he could dance, to which he said he couldn't, so Les was a little less surprised when he received the choreography notes for the dance he was to perform.

Sid and Eddie said they would do their usual thing here and there, as did the Dame, Ken Wilson, who despite being seventy and completely deaf, insisted on opening the show with his usual routine. After a couple of rehearsals, Les threw away his script when he realised all his part actually comprised of was swinging in on a rope, singing a song, firing an arrow and having a fight with the Sheriff of Nottingham.

Les swore he'd never do panto again; *Babes in the Wood* wasn't a pleasurable experience from start to finish. But he was performing a sketch on the Children's Royal Variety when he met a Jon Conway, who offered him Hook in *Peter Pan*, which proved to be a far more professional affair, and Les did panto every year after that.

He began writing a wine column for the Sunday Mirror, which led to a wine slot, *Grantham's Grapes,* on *This Morning.* The articles had initially been written by someone else, but when Les felt they were leaning too much on his *EastEnders* fame, and wanted to be taken seriously in the wine game, he successfully requested to begin writing them himself. For each column, he'd be flown all over the world to visit vineyards and winemakers. This went on for several years, until he was asked to write an investigative piece exposing corruption in the wine industry; 'It just wasn't me, I never claimed to be a wine expert, I just knew what I liked and wanted to take some of the snobbery away from it.'

Les was still trying to get other projects into development. He'd had an idea for a drama set on an oil rig, that he had pitched to Channel 4, and Peter Ansorge, the then head of drama, had liked it and commissioned a writer to come up with some drafts. Les had wanted to cast Michael Elphick as the villain, but he declined, not wanting to play against his type and to maintain his good guy image. As the project developed further, it became too expensive to pull off and was abandoned.

Zenith had acquired the rights to the *Duffy* books and wanted Les to play the lead, but the said he didn't think a series would do the material justice, and a film was the way to go. Zenith didn't agree and so that too was abandoned.

Determined to make something work for Les, Zenith commissioned Terry Johnson to write a series for him. *99-1* would star Les as Mick Raynor, a police officer caught up in a corruption enquiry, who goes undercover to bring down a criminal network. With a fantastic cast including Robert Carlyle, Robert Stephens, Danny Webb, Adie Allen and Niall Buggy, it was a great shoot, though it was nearly cut short on the first day. The scene required Les to drive a car at speed onto the platform of Kings Cross station and slam the brakes on, stopping inches from a train. The camera rolled and Les accelerated towards the edge of the platform. As he put his foot on the brake, nothing happened. As he got closer to the train, he wasn't slowing down, so pulled up the handbrake at the last minute, spinning the car and bringing it to a halt an inch from the edge. Fortunately, the camera operator hadn't run for cover and had kept recording, so a second take wasn't required, much to Les's relief.

The first series was a huge success and a second was commissioned after the first episode went out. Robert Stephens, however, wasn't well following a bad blood transfusion. He was also playing King Lear while they were filming, so was extremely tired. Les was shooting one scene with him, when Robert was struggling to say his lines, not because he didn't know them, but because he was in so much pain. As his health continued to decline, he was unable to appear in the second series and so was replaced by Frances Tomelty.

After two seasons, and in spite of great numbers, Carlton didn't renew *99-1* for a third season, and so it was back to the drawing board at Zenith. Les's next idea was a sci-fi drama about an alien invasion, titled *Who are You?*. He and Archie took the idea to Charles Denton at the BBC, who commissioned a script but by the time it had been written, Denton had moved on and the BBC decided not to pursue the project. They then took it to Nick Elliot, who had been head of LWT, but recently appointed head of drama for ITV. They pitched it to him as an ITV series, which then became *The Uninvited*.

Les then created another series, called *Bomber*, and left it with Archie to come up with a list of names of writers. He also starred alongside Roy Hudd in a tour of the play *Theft*, which received much critical acclaim.

One day, he received a call from his agent, telling him that Archie Tait had put out a casting call for actresses for film called *Bomber*. He contacted Archie, whom at that moment in time he hadn't heard from in a while, and asked what was going on, but Archie dismissed all of Les's questions. Allegedly, they had employed a writer who didn't like writing for a named actor and had also revised the project to make it posher, something Archie considered a more accurate depiction of the bomb squad; 'I'm pretty sure no cop actually walks the streets of San Francisco saying 'make my day, punk', but they managed to get a couple of successful films out of that, didn't they...'

Archie reassured Les that the director would give him a part if there was something in it he felt was suitable, but apparently the director didn't think there was anything suitable, because he never got another call. Les felt confused and blindsided; he'd created the idea for an original television series, Zenith had paid to develop the scripts and a writer had been paid to write the thing. In addition to that, Les said that Zenith had stood to make a substantial amount of money from it; 'I was getting fucked, and not in a good way!'

Les got back on the phone to his agent, who contacted Zenith to read them the riot act, demanding Les be credited and compensated appropriately, or they would attempt to stop the production. A deal was done and Les was rightfully credited as the author of the original idea on which the work was based.

Unfortunately, showbusiness is rife with this sort of conduct and *Bomber* wasn't the only such incident for Les. He'd been negotiating with the BBC about two other ideas of his, one called *Dead Files*, which followed a police team investigating old unsolved crimes and another, *Spent Force*, about a team of aging ex-policemen who form a vigilante group. Both of these projects were being discussed with the same BBC producer but after nearly two years of being given the run around, Les received a letter telling him they wouldn't be pursuing either production any further, but emphasised that should he see a production bearing any similarity in the future, the BBC had absolutely not stolen his ideas… *Waking The Dead* began airing in 2000 and ran for just over a decade, and *New Tricks* ran from 2003 until 2015.

A few film roles came up, including *Shadow Run*, alongside Michael Caine, and then Les's agent received an offer for a new television game show being devised, called *Fort Boyard*. Michael had initially tried to discourage Les from doing it, until his good friend Joe Pasquale called him to convince him otherwise. A mutual friend of theirs was directing and producing the series and so Les went to meet with him and Richard Holloway, the head of entertainment for Thames Television at the time. They showed Les a copy of the original French version of the show and he felt that everyone was a bit too nice in it, and it would be against his type. Fortunately, Thames agreed and much to the disappointment of the French, Les channelled Den and the show became a runaway hit.

Filmed at a marvellous Napoleonic fort off the Bay of Biscay, the crew were ferried by boat and helicopter for a three-days-on-three-days-off shoot. The programme ran for several years and amassed a cult daytime following, but its biggest fan, and the one that mattered most to Les, was Walter.

At the time of Fort Boyard's peak success, Walter was still busy helping with local elections and attempting to get a good friend of his into the position of local mayor. After the most recent local mayoral race, Les had travelled down to take Walter and his friend out for lunch at one of his favourite restaurants. Afterwards, when Les dropped him home, he told Walter he was looking a little tired, and to make sure he looked after himself. At this point, Adelaide had been moved to a home, so Walter had the place to himself. The next day, Les received a call from a girl that did some occasional ironing and housework for Walter, to say that she had arrived to find him naked, pouring boiling water on his cornflakes and having emptied a bag of sugar over the kitchen floor. Les phoned a friend of Walters that had a spare key and set off right away. By the time he arrived, Walter's friend was already at the house, but Walter was nowhere to be seen. After several hours driving around looking for him, Les decided to go back to the house and wait for him. He eventually turned up several more hours later, dressed in his best suit and overcoat; 'He looked completely confused to see us and said he didn't know what we were worrying about because he'd only popped out to the toilet in the garden. Given we hadn't had a toilet in our garden since 1947, this was cause for concern.'

Walter's friend promised to stop by the next day to check on him. A nurse arrived from Adelaide's nursing home, who'd seen Walter at one of the mayoral rallies and thinking he was looking tired, had also started to stop by regularly. Les phoned Jane to tell her he was going to spend the night at his dads and then went and fetched supper for Walter, the nurse and himself.

Walter had always been early to rise, never out of bed later than 6:30 a.m., so the next morning when he still hadn't come downstairs as eight o'clock approached, Les was on his way up to check on Walter when he heard an almighty bang. He ran into his room to find him having fallen over whilst trying to put his trousers on, but he insisted he was fine and would be down shortly. Apprehensively, Les went back downstairs and began to prepare breakfast when he then heard something being dragged across the floor upstairs. He went back up to Walter's room to find him trying to pull himself toward the stairs. Les phoned the doctor immediately, who came and confirmed that Walter had had a stroke and would need rest. At first, Jane insisted that Walter come to stay with them in Wimbledon, but his friends pointed out that he didn't know anyone other than Les there, and it might be better to find him a place in a home closer to his friends, so they could stop by regularly. After some phoning around, it turned out that the only home that had a place was the same one Adelaide was in; 'I was shocked there was only one space there, you'd have thought there would have been half a dozen!'

Needless to say, Walter didn't want to go there or be anywhere near Adelaide. Les phoned social services, and upon hearing Walter's name, they managed to find him a place in another home not far from his house. Les went to look it over with Walter's friend, and they decided it was the best thing for him. Les went to

Marks & Spencer and bought a new dressing gown and pyjamas for him, and some new clothes so he'd look sharp when Les would visit and take him for walks, and he could look and feel his best, even in his new condition and surroundings; 'It was so sad and pitiful to see this old man who until a week ago had been running around like a man half his age. It broke my heart to see him sat in the back of the ambulance, he just looked defeated.'

Les would travel to see Walter every day. He gave Les power of attorney and drew up a new will, including a clause that stipulated he didn't want Angela or Adelaide at his funeral; 'I understood it, but at the time it didn't even feel necessary because even there in the home, the notion of him dying seemed years away, it hadn't even really occurred.'

But within a few weeks, Walter began to deteriorate, and within a month was being spoon fed. Les and Jane had a family holiday booked to Australia to see Jane's parents but the day before they were due to leave, the home had phoned Les to say they didn't think Walter had long left and it would be best if Les came to be with him.

The following morning, still half asleep, Les answered the phone to the news that Adelaide had passed away. It was the nursing home calling him under the instructions of Angela, who had insisted that Les would be paying for the funeral. He phoned Adelaide's family and told them the news, as Angela shifted all responsibility to Les. He then got dressed and went to the funeral home to organise the funeral, and then to see Walter, to tell him the news.

Two days later, Jane took a call from the nursing home, again telling them that Walter was fading, and it would be best if Les came to be with him. Les had just arrived home from a night shoot when Jane told him, and they both drove straight to the home.

Les sat beside Walter and held his hand, knowing this time he was indeed on his way out. He told him it was time to get in his boat, as the ferryman was waiting for him and was going to take him to see his friends and family. As Les recited the names of those closest to him, a single tear rolled down Walter's cheek, he smiled and squeezed Les's hand. Les recalled a brief smell of burnt toast and with that, Walter died.

Jane drove them home, Les sat in silence. When they got to the house, Les went out into the back garden and lit a cigarette and as he looked up at the night sky above, saw a lone light travelling. He said it stopped, then got brighter and then vanished. He said that was his sign, his way of knowing that Walter had reached his final destination and was safe now. He also knew that he had lost his best friend, the only person who had stood by him unconditionally. This was a father who, when he found out his son had taken the life of another man, stood by his side, always, and told him while he couldn't condone what he'd done, he was there with him, and together, they would find a way to move forward. That's quite a man, a father and a friend…

Les went indoors and repeated the calls he had had to make only two days before, only this time about his father. Les said that Adelaide's family were far more devastated by the news of Walter's death than their own sisters, and they promised to try and travel over for his funeral, though as they were to be on different days, Les discouraged them and said there was no need.

One of Walter's friends wore his uniform to lead other members of his regiment in the funeral procession, accompanied by a lone piper playing *Danny Boy*. After the service, the funeral cortege drove through Aldershot, where flags were flown at half-mast and the staff of Boots the chemist stood outside to bow their heads. At the crematorium, Frank Sinatra's *My Way* was played and as Walter was about to begin his final journey behind the curtain, against his expressed wishes, Angela walked in, threw a single rose on the coffin and walked back out again, much to the disgust of the mourners.

The funeral was important to Les, having not been able to attend his brother Philips years earlier. It had been in 1986, at the height of Les's fame when he'd received a call from Adelaide, demanding to know why he hadn't been to see his brother Philip. Apparently, and completely unbeknownst to Les, he was in the hospital suffering from 'some type of cancer'. Having only seen him a few weeks prior, this was a little hard to believe, so Les headed straight for the hospital, only to be told Philip had checked himself out. When he got to Philips flat, it was obvious that it wasn't cancer. He took one look at this suddenly frail and small man and could tell right away it was AIDS. He was struggling to move about, cold and hungry, so Les went and got some groceries in for him, cooked him a hot meal and did his best to make him a little more comfortable.

Within a month, Philip was admitted back into hospital. Unfortunately, word got out and the press were there, photographing a dying man on his deathbed. He had called Les after that and asked if he wouldn't mind not attending his funeral as he didn't want it turned into a media circus. It felt awful to have to agree with his wishes, but Les knew it was the right and respectful thing to do. So when Philip passed, their sister Angela naturally couldn't pass up the opportunity to sell the story to the papers that Les had abandoned his own brother in his hour of need and furthermore, so awful was he, that he couldn't even be bothered to show up to the funeral.

For Walter, a do at the British Legion club followed and he was given a proper send off, before everybody went their own separate ways again; 'I never really came to terms with losing my dad, I could never really get my head around how someone so generous and kind and loving could just not be there anymore. Without him, I've always felt something missing inside me, beside me.'

CHAPTER TWELVE

As the twentieth anniversary of *EastEnders* approached, the show once again reached out to Les. After reassurances about storylines, he agreed to a meeting with Louise Berridge, the executive producer at the time. After much back and forth, a deal was agreed and they met again, this time at a Chinese restaurant around the corner from the studios in Elstree. The BBC press office had tipped off the paparazzi, so Les had to stand outside looking pleased to see the photographers.

A week later, another meeting followed with Colin Wratten, the producer of his first block of episodes, Louise Berridge, Letitia Dean and Nigel Harman; 'Nigel and I got on like a house on fire, and being with Tish was like no time had passed at all, it was like I'd never been away.'

Penned by one of *EastEnders* most respected writers, Sarah Phelps delivered the scripts to Les, who thought they were wonderful.

For the first time in nearly fifteen years, the great Den Watts returned to Albert Square. Stalwarts like Adam Woodyatt, Wendy Richard, Pat St Clements and of course June Brown welcomed him back with open arms, as did several crew members who'd been there since the beginning.

His first scene comprised of walking out from behind a plant in Angie's Den and whispering the immortal line, 'Hello Princess'. After a long, arduous day, he did the scene; 'I stepped out, said the line and as soon as the director yelled 'cut!', the place erupted in applause. God only knows what would have happened if I'd have jumped out and delivered Hamlet!'

The next episode, a two-hander between Les and Letitia, was just over thirty pages; not an uncommon length for scripts that would have to be learned word-perfect, nightly before getting up early and trying to beat Laila Morse to be first in in the morning. Billy Murray once joked that he was going to buy his script a wig, as he'd regularly spend more evenings curled up in bed with it than he would his wife. If acting on a soap doesn't make you able to digest a script in a timely manner, nothing will.

After a couple of months on screen, Den took a trip back to Spain, when in fact Les was in Ireland doing pantomime. It was a welcome break from the combination of having hit the ground running on *EastEnders* and a growing frustration and distain for the younger cast members; 'They just didn't take it seriously, they had no respect for the show or its history, it's heritage. Most days, just turning up on time seemed impossible and when they were there, you could tell it was just one massive inconvenience to their social lives. They'd have all rather been at PR events cutting ribbons at nightclubs, but they were all too thick and self-absorbed to realize that without *EastEnders*, they wouldn't have had any of those opportunities!'

This was a moot point for Les, who could never avoid bringing it up every time we'd discuss *EastEnders*; shooting would regularly overrun because of the younger cast members lack of punctuality, inability to learn lines or their ruining scenes by attempting to rush through them so they could get out early. It was much of the same frustrations that had made him quit the first time.

That Christmas, Jane took the boys to Australia to stay with her family while Les appeared as 'Dirty Rat' in pantomime in Belfast. It was, as usual, a huge success, and after the run, Les joined Jane and the kids for a short break in South Africa before returning once more to Walford; 'Things couldn't have been going better... so I guess I should have known better.'

Les was set up in a sting by a tabloid. That is a black and white matter of fact. This is how tabloids work. They sit in their offices having meetings actually based around 'who's life can we ruin this week?' Since the phone hacking scandal was exposed, social media now makes their job even easier. For example, when a new actor joins *EastEnders* or a new contestant joins *Love Island*, it is the job of a team of 'journalists' to dig as deep and as far back as they can in your online presence to find absolutely anything that they can use to destroy you and your career, to drive you to the brink of bankruptcy or suicide, preferably both. Or, they don't even actually have to find anything, they can just make it up; whatever suits the narrative they wish to portray. That is what sells newspapers.

So, at some point, a meeting would have occurred in Fleet Street where a team decided 'Leslie Grantham is on top right now, how do we ruin him' and all kinds of brainstorming would have gone on and eventually, the sting that ensued was put into place.

By his own admission, his discovery of the internet came very late in life and was certainly a revelation to him. Les was always more hesitant talking about the online sex scandal than he was about the death of Felix Reese, because he accepted all responsibility for the latter, he knew it was his fault and he never forgave himself, and rightly so. But the sex scandal was a complete stitch up, regardless of his own stupidity in falling for it.

What started as a natural interest in pornography became his way of filling time between takes when he'd be in his dressing room for hours waiting to be called back to set. By his own admission, he spent too much time looking at adult material and in online chat rooms, but the early red flags appeared when he started getting messages from people who claimed they'd spoken with him earlier, at which point he realised his computer had been hacked.

A couple of weeks later, a tabloid ran a story about a woman he'd met in a tearoom years ago, who was now claiming she and Les had been lovers for near two years. The first Les heard about this was when another newspaper called him for a comment. He contacted his agent, and the police were promptly involved when it was discovered a journalist had been claiming to be Les in order to obtain phone bills from his phone carrier and calling his bank to obtain copies of his bank statements. In case you're in any doubt, journalists continue today to obtain stories using methods including this.

Around this time, Les also received an email from a woman claiming to work at Yorkshire Television. She had said she was a fan of his and requested a signed photo. A few days later she emailed him again to thank him for the photo and they continued to exchange more emails pertaining to working in television. By this time, Les had googled her and everything appeared to check out; Yorkshire Television, weather presenter, etc. She then introduced Les to her friend 'Amanda' via Messenger, a dancer from Sheffield; 'How I didn't see it coming by then is beyond me, I was a complete and utter fool.'

Quite. A flirtatious, attractive twenty-something dancer playing to an actor's vanity, trying to convince him to converse with her via a web camera. Each time they spoke, she would up the intimacy and the questions would become more and more probing, moving from sex to *EastEnders*. As he recalled this out loud, we both couldn't help but see how painfully obviously it all was, in that wonderful thing called hindsight.

And just like that, Amanda vanished. It was timed perfectly. It was Les's birthday and he and Jane were leaving the house when a reporter turned up with the newspaper and article. It was 1985 all over again, as the house was besieged by paparazzi and journalists. Naturally it was the perfect time for his sister Angela to resurface, talking to any paper that would listen to her. There were plenty of them, obviously.

Consumed by guilt as he tried to lie his way out of the mess, Les tried to slash his wrists with a Stanley knife but unfortunately the blade was so old, it was blunt, and he struggled to even break the skin. He contemplated slashing is throat but then came up with what he thought was a better plan. He went into the garden and using one of the children's skipping ropes, tied a noose and attached it to a tree. As he jumped, the branch broke, hitting him on the head. Not to be deterred, he tied the skipping rope to a drainpipe and jumped again, not having taken into account newer skipping ropes are made from nylon and are inclined to stretch, so he just landed on the lawn.

Les returned to work two days later, where he was fined by the BBC but told there would be no further punishment, at least from the BBC; the papers would take care of the rest. Although Les was relatively safe while at Elstree again, Jane and the children were hounded mercilessly, and it was all the more distressing for Danny, the most vulnerable of the family. The home phone would ring non-stop, either with journalists wanting a quote or people wanting to tell Les what they thought of him. Residents at Elstree were renting their spare rooms out to photographers desperate to get closer to the set. The same photographers would also offer Les's neighbours' money to stand in their garden, just to try and get photos of Jane and the kids.

The tipping point for Les was GMTV turning up with a reporter and cameraman and ringing the doorbell repeatedly. When Les told them where to go, they obviously kept ringing the doorbell until Danny innocently opened the door, and they then tried to get a quote from a ten-year-old with Down's syndrome. I'd be reluctant to call this a new low as I have another friend who was in a similar predicament and *The Sun* newspaper sent a helicopter to his house to take photographs through his children's bedroom windows. It's all in a day's work, in their morally bankrupt world.

It was the children suffering from his actions that was too much and he attempted suicide again, this time by trying to drown himself in a pond on Wimbledon Common, but it turned out to not be deep enough for the job in hand; 'I accepted that even at suicide, I was crap, so I'd best just get on with it.'

After that, Les moved into a flat nearer the studios, to try and deflect the attention from Jane and the children ,but this naturally only resulted in headlines claiming he'd been kicked out of the matrimonial home; 'They were offering the residents in the building cash if they'd let them take photos of their flats, but luckily they were so offended by the papers description of their homes as 'dingy' and 'squalid', they all told them where to go.'

Whatever Les did resulted in some kind of headline. He went to see his cousin and the papers decided that was his latest affair. It wasn't long before a mole inside the BBC was found, who had been leaking Les's schedule to the paparazzi. *EastEnders* for the most part were very supportive, however the whole saga was a firm reminder that no matter how close you think someone is, they will always believe what they read in the press, especially when it's about someone else, and so a lot of people abandoned him.

Eventually Les was summoned to see Mal Young; 'Mal was the kind of producer that couldn't wait to do a photoshoot with his girlfriend for Hello! magazine. He wasn't liked by most and made life there very difficult for a lot of people, mostly just for his own pleasure.'

Mal, although admitting he fully understood the scandal had been the result of a tabloid set up, informed Les that one of the younger members of cast had complained that they felt he should be punished further, and so Mal was obligated to suspend him.

And that was the end of that. After his suspension, Les returned to Albert Square for what would be the final time. By now, the scripts were just as late as the younger cast members and when they did arrive, much like the young cast, they weren't great. Les was often vocal to me in his disappointment and frustration with the new breed of actors, especially members of the Ferreira family, but also Jessie Wallace and Shane Richie, and their obsession with fame over substance, observing how quickly their egos would inflate after just a few days in Walford. Les had so much love for *EastEnders*. He valued and respected the dedication, craftsmanship and love Julia had put into its creation. He appreciated the work of the long serving crew, and of the actors that turned up off book, but the kids that waltzed in and suddenly thought they were god's gift, he had no time for, and it really grated on him.

It was one day during his final blocks that he remembered standing in the carpark between takes, having a cigarette and seeing Louise Berridge. She was visibly different, happy, as if the weight of the world had been lifted from her shoulders. It wasn't until the end of their conversation that Les realised she had just resigned. He had a soft spot for Louise, and it meant a lot to him how kindly and respectfully she treated him. He saw a lot of Julia in her. From a viewer's perspective, I shared Les's opinion that Louise was responsible for one of the best eras of the show and not until or since Diederick Santer has the *EastEnders* had another executive producer who was so like Julia, in so many ways.

Louise was superseded by Kathleen Hutchinson, appropriately named 'The Hatchet' by the press. She'd come over from *Holby City*, also filmed at Elstree, and much like Mal Young, had some questionable views on what was wrong with the show and how to fix it. To say Les disagreed with her would be an understatement, yet true to form, he never made a fuss.

On the day Les was called to her office to discuss his characters new storylines, he knew it was time to go. Kathleen was responsible for introducing Billy Murray as gangster Johnny Allen and in keeping with that, wanted to move Den into equal territory. Les, having felt he had grown up with his share of real Dens, and combined with his protectiveness over the character, disagreed. As Les said, those kinds of Jack-the-lads are always big fish in their little ponds, duckers-and-divers, not Don Vito Corleone; 'The middle-class execs that wrote the stuff were obsessed with the gangsters. What was supposed to be representative of a microcosm of working-class East London was being written by upper-class writers in Holland Park wine bars, it was never going to end well.'

Protective of Den, a character he considered to be one of the treasures he cherished the most in all his life, Les couldn't agree; 'I'm Dirty Den and there's not a day that goes by that I won't be proud to say that, and not only was I a part of something so special, I was one of its icons. I just couldn't destroy him like that.'

His final day and send off were an emotional one and I know he didn't really want to go; that was evident from his tears.

CHAPTER THIRTEEN

Away from *EastEnders*, Les finally got to return to two other loves; writing and theatre, especially pantomime. There's a lot of snobbery around pantomime, but not only is it incredibly lucrative, it's a wonderful art form and a British institution. Les thought it was absolutely fabulous, and it brought him a lot of joy. He loved directing, every bit as much as performing and in his remaining years built a very good reputation as being one of the best there was.

After what happened with *New Tricks* and *Waking the Dead,* writing was something he largely did for himself as a hobby, and later when he became sick, it would become a form of therapy. He had the attitude that if anything came from it, great, but if not, he was quite happy tapping away on his own.

Les also did a couple of low budget films; the likes of *Mob Handed, Deadtime* and *The Game,* which for a while, he was hopeful would never see the light of day. All of them were, by his own admission, 'utter shit'.

The strain that the sex scandal had put on Les and Jane's marriage was never really repaired.

In 2010, he was offered the lead role of John Stuart in the Bulgarian series *The English Neighbour*, based upon the book by the same name by Mihail Veshim. The tabloids obviously lapped up the fact that he 'had resorted to' appearing in the show, as if it were some further fall from grace, but it was very well received, and he was rewarded for the risk he took. He also fell in love with Bulgaria and the city of Sofia.

After years of friendship, Les and I finally embarked on our first film together in 2012. Pre-production had been plagued by casting issues and the usual development hell, but eventually we rolled in the late summer. I'd gone through this motion many times; you know an actor personally or you've approached them outside of their agent, yet you still have to pretend neither is the case when you approach the agent for the first time, or they fear they might have missed out on a cheque somewhere. We met in Plateau restaurant in Canary Wharf, one of our favourite spots and a deal was done. That film, even though it would later be plagued by further issues, was one of my career highlights; shooting a scene in my own penthouse high above Canary Wharf between Billy Murray and Leslie Grantham, I couldn't help but have a huge smile on my face the whole time. In between takes, I remember Les and Billy sitting together. Billy was having his make-up done so in order to compensate, said to Les in front of the whole crew 'what the fuck made you do *The Jeremy Kyle Show*' to which, as quick as a flash, Les replied, 'Ten grand.'

I'd known Billy a decade at this point, we were good friends and close neighbours in both London's Docklands and in Bodrum, Turkey. I loved Billy very much and looked at him as a father figure, but he's a man's man and not the kind you talk about your feelings with. Les, however, wore his heart on his sleeve and we would regularly confide in each other.

Billy was brought in at the last minute to replace another actor; ironically one who had the same attitude of having attended the Clint Eastwood School of Acting *aka* 'I'll say it with a look'. Don't get me wrong, obviously Clint Eastwood is a master. But the look on Les's face as Billy attempted to suggest he'd erase pages of dialogue between the two characters and indeed 'say it with a look' when Les had clearly learnt not only his lines but Billy's and the scenes either side which didn't even involve him was a picture. I don't disagree completely with the ethos. Sometimes less is more, but there's a time and a place.

Between takes, he was the consummate professional that his friends and colleagues had always described. His insecurities were also very clear; every other question was whether I was happy with his performance, was that take okay, was that look alright? It was an odd combination of being so off book and exactly as any director could want for, and he questioned it all. Nothing he ever did was good enough for himself, and he always felt he could do better. 'Do you want to go again?' clearly meant 'I think I can do it better', though

I'd rather hear that, than 'You see all this dialogue you've taken months to write… I think I'll say it with a look…'

In the wake of the Levinson Inquiry in early 2013, Les was amongst those acknowledged and compensated for having had their phone hacked by The News of the World, and a few weeks later his marriage, estranged for several years, was dissolved with the judge ruling that Jane's behaviour had become so abhorrent that Les could no longer reasonably be expected to live with her. Thirty-one years of marriage were over.

Les and I went on to do another two short films together that year. The first, *The Factory*, he adored because it came him terrific range, and the second, *Leslie,* gave us the chance to really spend some time with each other. For *The Factory*, interiors were filmed in London but for the exteriors, on his recommendation, we travelled to Sofia in Bulgaria, where he was settling in just fine and he was in his element, showing me around between filming.

The second short, entitled *Leslie*, was a mockumentary, with Les playing a fictionalised version of himself, forced to take a road trip with his estranged daughter to see his dying ex-wife. As it was largely improvised, we went over a set of rules between ourselves for me to impart to the actress playing his daughter as to what was off limits; the only thing really being Felix Reese. He was a great sport about the whole thing, he loved being back in the Lake District. The project went on to do well on the festival circuit and it held a special place in both our hearts.

When Les returned to London, between filming, things were not as rosy. He was, by his own admission, flat out broke and homeless. When in England, he'd either spend his time on the couch of a friend's house in West London or in my spare room.

Before his annual foray into panto, he took part in a very amusing little play entitled *HollyEnders Street*, a kind of tongue-in-cheek homage to all the major soaps, with stalwarts like Graham Cole and Lee Otway, though the highlight for him was working with Kev Orkian, whom he frequently collaborated with in panto.

Through sheer hard graft, Les was able to make the permanent move to Bulgaria and each time I visited him there, he didn't have a care in the world. It was like visiting another person, I never saw him as happy and relaxed as he was there. There's a huge film industry in Sofia, some major studios are there and Les would regularly get background work in all those Van Damme and Nicholas Cage movies that are churned out, and the likes of *The Expendables*. It was a lovely way for him to be on a set and to work consistently but have none of the attention and pressure that came from the tabloids when on *EastEnders*.

He also continued to write and developed a screenplay for a proper old school detective thriller, akin to *Broadchurch*, called *Maybe Tomorrow*, which my production company acquired the rights to and is currently in development on. He also began work on a children's book, which, although he was modest about, he aspired it would be the next *Lord of the Rings* or *Harry Potter*. I remember being at home in Los Angeles when he sent me the link to his appearance on *This*

Morning, as he proudly promoted the finished book, *Jack Bates and the Wizard's Spell*, to Ruth and Eamon. Unfortunately, we both knew by this point, that all that glitters, is not golden.

The following chapter was by far the hardest of both this book and of any other pages I've had to write in my career. While the majority of this book is based upon my recollection of conversations Les and I exchanged in specific places and times, the following required having to reread and rehear specific text messages, emails and voicemails that were incredibly painful to revisit; as I did so with each one, I relived the emotions I'd felt when I first received them. It was only in doing so for the purpose of this book that I was reminded just how long he battled his illness, but also how long it had been since I'd heard his voice; both hurt in equal measures.

CHAPTER FOURTEEN

I'd been living in Los Angeles for three years by the time 2016 arrived, and my first son Jude had been born the previous November. My fiancé, Jude and I had just moved into a new apartment, our business was doing well, I was getting back on my feet and Les and I were emailing and calling each other regularly. He was happy in Bulgaria, always telling me about his latest encounter with Van Damme or Bruce Willis at the studios just outside of Sofia. For both of us, life was finally resembling good and trouble free, so we should have both known better.

Then Les sent me an email that at first started just like any other; weather, films, wine, the state of British television… and that he had been having trouble breathing at night for the last month, and he'd had 'a few scares' that had really bothered him, so when he was next in London, he'd visit the doctors and get it checked out.

Both the NHS and a friend of a friend on Harley Street misdiagnosed Les, but for the ripe old sum of twelve pounds upon returning to Bulgaria, he was diagnosed with emphysema. As he said those words, every cigarette I'd seen him smoke sprung to mind, flashing before my eyes. Every story he'd ever told me somehow revolved around them, but my fiancé put my mind at ease, and I was convinced that this wasn't anything that couldn't be cured.

A couple of months later, he text me to tell me that upon visiting London and informing them of the Bulgarian diagnosis, the NHS had confirmed not only the Emphysema, but also that he had lung cancer. He would have to await further test results to see if it could be treated. He apologised for not having the courage to have called me to tell me over the phone. I think I kept the news to myself for an hour or so before my fiancé asked me what was wrong, and I broke down in tears. I can remember it being one of those occasions that you can literally feel your heart break in two, and not a day goes by when you can't recall that physical feeling. She knew he was the only friend I had, but also how much he meant to me. She was a survivor of cancer herself, so I know she knew the gravity of the situation and she knew what Les had stood by me through.

A few weeks after, he confided that he had to have six rounds of chemotherapy over eighteen weeks, or without, he'd have three months to live. Even then, his good humour shone through as he requested a hat as a Christmas gift.

He was, to use the turn of phrase, sick as a dog, as is anyone, during chemotherapy and radiotherapy. His immune system, blood count and temperature were all over the place, and any time he thought something was working, it wasn't and there was a delay. Any time something was nearly clear, it wasn't.

A month later, he endured a second round of chemotherapy and if there was a virus or side effect he was susceptible to, he suffered it. He started to lose the hair he was so proud of. I'd never seen him without perfectly groomed, swept back hair – right at the end, that little comb he carried around with him in his pocket was there, and he was perfectly quaffed and slicked back, even when it was just a few wisps remaining.

He went to Bulgaria completely drained of energy, not only physically from the treatment, but emotionally from the speed at which the diagnosis had hit him. He spent that Christmas and saw in 2017 in Bulgaria but still struggled with breathing. He tried to pass the symptoms off as being down to the cold climate there, but I soon persuaded him to return to London when he developed an infection in his gums, and he undertook four weeks of radiotherapy.

I was about to marry my fiancé and Les had been gladly accepted the position of best man, but we'd both been kidding ourselves about his condition and ability to even contemplate such a feat. I married Tiffany, the love of my life, the day before Les's birthday. His message to me, in his usual humour, informed me that he couldn't have travelled if he'd have wanted to, not for physical ailment, but because his passport photo resembled 'The Great Den Watts' and he in fact looked closer to the illegitimate child of Mr Magoo and a tortoise.

A couple of months later, he was planning to leave Sofia to return to England fulltime, still blaming the air quality of Bulgaria, but we both knew it was a lifetime of the cigarettes. For Christ sakes, he'd been having treatment for lung cancer for over a year, it was nothing to do with how cold it was in Bulgaria.

When he returned to London, he was told his lungs were improving but the cancer had now spread to his spine, and more chemotherapy and radiotherapy took its toll on him. Just before Christmas he was told his treatment was finished, but not before he directed three sperate pantomime productions and starred in a fourth. He knew then, exactly what was going to happen, and he knew exactly what he was doing, executing his escape plan.

In 2018, I was asked to write and direct a straight-to-DVD gangster film. It wasn't the kind of film I'd usually choose to make, very much painting-by-numbers, but it was a film with a distribution deal already done and most importantly, it was a chance to work with Les one last time. It must have been the coldest day of the year, stood in the middle of Highgate Wood when he arrived on set, perfectly groomed and dressed, but he could barely walk. He knew his lines perfectly and delivered the scene in one perfect take and then, hunched over, shuffled to me and asked, 'was that alright, do you want me to do it again, I can do it better.' I let him make a big fuss in making out he was demanding a car to pick him up and drive him home, but in reality, it was because he couldn't make it to the corner of the street, let alone back to unit base, he was in agony. How he even turned up was beyond me, let alone speak his lines.

It was during that shoot, that Les had been over for one last chance at experimental chemotherapy, not the film, and he didn't feel he could let me down and knew how much working together properly one last time meant. The cancer was in his lungs, spine, stomach, everywhere…

We had other projects we were always writing together, but this was going to be our last time together on a working set and we both knew that. Before I was due for filming the following day, I went with him to hospital at stupid-o'clock in the morning, where we were told his blood count was too low for the rest of the treatment. I put him on a train to Gatwick to catch a flight back to Bulgaria and I headed to Bethnal Green to watch the crew whisper amongst themselves about my article that the producer had been circulating, and then listen to them tell me how cold they were and ask what time lunch was.

A week later, Les's blood hadn't improved and so he still wasn't well enough for more chemotherapy. I remember texting him after his latest appointment and asking how how'd gotten on, and he just text me back with 'sorry… one week.'

It was the thirteenth of April when he called me to tell me he desperately needed help, though it was for the most part hard to understand what he was saying, as his speech was so slurred from medication. This was obviously more shocking to me, given only days ago he'd been, albeit in pain, not only completely coherent but delivered a three-page monologue word-for-word, off book. The texts and phone calls became more incoherent as he lost the use of his arms and legs, very quickly becoming bed ridden.

Bringing Les from Bulgaria to West Middlesex Hospital was pretty much a military operation. It required begging the British Embassy in Sofia, no easy feat on its own, before a thirty-six-hour ride via Serbia in an ambulance that looked like it had been in service since Les's time in the army. When his friend Jamie emailed me to say he was receiving visitors, it had taken a few days for him to be drained of the medications he'd been fed in Bulgaria and he eventually, thankfully, regained the use of his arms and legs.

When I arrived, Jamie greeted me in the hospital lobby. As he led me up to the ward, he seemed remarkably chipper, telling me that Les had improved, he was in good spirits, but that I should be prepared. Seeing him in that room, in such a state is a bit of a blur. My wife had a friend who'd died of cancer the year before, and to raise awareness of how this cruel disease can strike at any age, his family had released an image of him in his final moments holding his young child. When I saw Les, it knocked me for six. As I say, the only way I can describe it would be if a charity wanted to release a photo of someone suffering from lung cancer with the intention of discouraging you from so much as looking at a packet of cigarettes. I barely recognised him, yet he was in such high spirits. But he was skin and bones, and it was the beginning of an undignified end to an incredible man. His eyes were sunken, his hair as good as gone and his skin like rice paper. But my god, he never let that quick wit drop for a moment, and right beside his bed was his little comb.

He was surrounded by a couple of friends; an older gentleman whom I can't quite recall, although I know they had done a television show together, Jaime of course, Kev, who'd starred in many a pantomime and *HollyEnders Street* with him, and a relative of Les's girlfriend, who'd travelled over from Bulgaria. Les's girlfriend, having watched him deteriorate in Bulgaria, decided that she couldn't be there for the end as it was too painful for her, and Les, and all of us completely understood. I do know they loved each other and very made each other very happy. The older gentleman, whom I struggle to recall, was, like me, uncomfortable and at a loss of what to say to Les, we were so shocked by his appearance. It was a bizarre atmosphere, only because Les kept making jokes which were very, very funny and we were all in stitches, but we'd be promptly hit by pains of guilt, because all we actually wanted to do was cry. Even though it was the first time we'd met, Kev was very good at reading the room and bringing the mood up every time I think he could see I was about to lose it. I didn't want to laugh. It was one of those moments when you wish the ground would just swallow you up. All I wanted to do was cry, hug Les tightly and tell him how much I loved him, but he looked so fragile that had I tried, I might have broken him. So instead, I tried to be cheerful, but inside I was hoping that he couldn't see my heart was breaking all over again.

Over the next few days, a list of people he'd carefully selected came to see him. He was happy to see all of them, with the exception of his ex-wife Jane, whom he'd requested didn't know what was happening, but someone had called her anyway. No one from

EastEnders came; he had no relationship with any of them and had nothing but bitterness toward Anita Dobson, having never forgiven her for speaking to the papers during his sex scandal.

A week later, it was decided that Les should be moved to nearby Brinsworth House, a wonderful nursing and retirement home for people in the entertainment industry run by the Royal Variety Charity; the likes of Norman Wisdom and Thora Hird have passed there. Up until this point, the news had managed to be contained to Les's inner circle, but inevitably someone leaked the news to the press that he was at deaths door.

He really was. Confined to the chair in his room, he called several of us to tell us he was standing out in the garden at Brinsworth, as it had been permanently closed down and he was waiting for a bus back to Bulgaria. I went to visit him the next day and we watched *Casablanca* together while he narrated with his behind-the-scenes trivia. When the film finished, the nurse came into the room and asked him if he wanted lunch, but all he could manage was sorbet. He looked at me and told me just wanted to 'fucking die', as he was so tired, and in so much pain. He told me Jane had been to see him the day before, to tell him that she still hated him. He spoke of his regret and remorse for the people he'd hurt, and the lives he'd ruined. We began watching an old re-run of *The Champions* and he waxed lyrical for a moment about the good old days of television, and how people don't dress properly anymore. Then he apologised, and said he needed to sleep. I held his hand and kissed him on the forehead, I told him I loved him. He said it back and apologised again, before quoting one of Bogart's lines from *Casablanca*, followed by one of his trademark winks; 'Where I'm going, you can't follow.'

I left, promising to return the next day. The morning after, I received word that Jane had requested no more visitors, which was frustrating for two reasons; she couldn't stand him and until a few days ago they'd had nothing to do with each other since the divorce, and furthermore, the next day I was due to travel to Leicester for a film shoot and was terrified that I wouldn't get to see him again. The staff at Brinsworth House were apologetic, appalled at Jane's behaviour.

It was the end of the day on the 13th of June 2018, and I'd just wrapped filming for the day. I phoned Brinsworth House and was told Les was in a bad way, so I said I'd head back. When I told them where I was coming from, they gently told me that I was unlikely to make it, and I was best staying put. A friend of mine phoned me and offered to drive from Surrey to Leicester, a gesture I'll always remember, but it wouldn't have gotten me there any quicker.

The next day, I spoke with a mutual friend and he told me that Les was putting up a fight, so with only vague relief, I went about another days filming. I was only due to film for four days in Leicester, so with this news, I was now convinced I'd be able to make it back if I left as soon as I wrapped, in two days' time. Given that every time Les had been told how long he had over the last three years had been wrong, I slept a little better that night knowing he was hanging in there.

EPILOGUE

I never saw Les again. His ex-wife ensured he was alone when he passed, just after 10 a.m. on my birthday, 15th June 2018. I was stood on set in the middle of a council estate in Leicester when one of his good friends called me to tell me the news. Just like that, my best friend wasn't there anymore. I stood in the carpark and cried for over an hour and then, just like Les would have done, I went back to work.

That evening, I had a drink in the hotel we were staying at with one of the actors, the very kind and talented Charlie Woodward, and it seemed as though all that was on the television in the bar was news of Les's death; all the channels continuously played that famous clip of Den handing Angie the divorce papers. That's the funny thing about having a famous friend pass; they're immortalised in film, so to say you never see them again is a peculiar thing.

The next day, news of his passing was on the front page of every paper and, as always, anyone he'd barely bumped into, let alone never met, was spouting nonsense to any journalist that would listen. The producer of the film we'd made together, having already passed on details of his condition to the Sunday Mirror after private conversations with me, inevitably used his death to promote the film, even asking if I could get his girlfriend into Les's funeral, as it would be a 'great photo opportunity for her.' Les had loathed the man; having met him only twice and never one to suffer fools, he was quick to advise 'do one film with that man, and then move on, treat him like a steppingstone before he treats you like shit.'

In the weeks that followed, those that had been closest to him were shut out. He'd made arrangements for his own funeral, but they were contested by his family, who couldn't help letting him know how much they loathed him by arranging a private ceremony that none of his friends were permitted to attend. He was cremated and then the ashes were handed back to the very friends the family had banned from attending, and it was our responsibility to arrange for his final resting place. While I struggle to forgive or condone it, I understand why Jane acted the way she did toward Les; she endured years of humiliation because of his self-destructive behaviour, but there was no reason to treat the friends that loved him so cheaply, especially those of us for whom he'd done and meant so much.

Grief is a hurtful reminder that sometimes a person can have such a profound impact on your life that their departure is a wound time doesn't always heal; perhaps it's not meant to, or you'd forget all the truly invaluable lessons you learnt from them, or the wonderful memories you shared. It hurts to write something and not be able to send it over to him for his usual wry notes. It hurts to not have him tell me to keep going or to check I'm okay. Times like my wedding anniversary were when I could have done with one of his calls. What those things meant to me were immeasurable, because he was the only person that did them and now without them, I'm hard pushed to imagine a time when for at least thirty seconds of every day that won't break my heart. I struggle to articulate what it feels like to know the only person who had your back through the toughest fight of your life simply isn't there anymore, especially when you're still in that fight nearly a decade later. I can tell you it's bloody hard to get out of bed in the morning and keep fighting, but I do because I remember all the things he taught me. I remember his loyalty, his empathy, his humbleness, his patience and his resilience.

Whenever we were both in town together, and *Casablanca* was showing at The Prince Charles Cinema, we'd go and see it. I don't visit London often anymore but travelled there recently for a friend's book launch. When booking my train ticket, I checked the listings for the Prince Charles Cinema to see if anything worth seeing was showing later in the day, and of course, *Casablanca* was. I bought two tickets, one for him and one for me. Only as I went to enter the cinema did I recall the last time I had seen the movie was with Les, a few days before he left. While we had watched it, he had spoken of taking solace in dying in the same way Bogart had, and in that, he felt that he had 'made it'. The black dog returned to me with his crippling weight on my chest, and I was overwhelmed with the grief, anger and immense sadness I had felt when I was told he'd gone and with that, realised I couldn't bring myself to watch it anymore; not without him, but without being reminded of him in a way that still hurts my heart immeasurably. I dearly hope one day to be able to watch it again with that selfless perspective the ending instils, when the comfort that he's no longer in pain overrides the selfishness of my anger and hurt that he's no longer here for me. But until then, I know I can't follow him where he's gone.

If there's one thought I'd like to leave you with, something that I've not only learned from Les, but from everything that has happened to me in my life thus far, it's this; think back to the last conversation you had with someone you love. Ask yourself whether you would you be okay if that was, indeed, your last conversation. We're really only here for such a short, precious amount of time, and we take that for granted all too often. Make sure you're okay with the possibility that any conversation you have could be your last, in our fragile world of uncertainty. If you have anyone in your life that you love, be it your partner, your husband, your wife, your children, your dog, your grandmother or your best friend, tell them you love them.

I'm not particularly proud of many things in a life already full of mistakes, but I am proud to be the father of my children, and I am proud to have called Leslie Grantham my best friend.

Printed in Great Britain
by Amazon

31455156R00106